Hampton-Brown

edge™

Level Ⓑ TEACHER'S EDITION

Grammar & Writing Practice Book

NATIONAL GEOGRAPHIC   Hampton-Brown

Acknowledgment

Cover Art: *Night Voyage*, 2006, Patssi Valdez. Acrylic on canvas, 36"x48", courtesy of Patricia Correia Gallery, Santa Monica, California.

National Geographic School Publishing
Hampton–Brown
P.O. Box 223220
Carmel, California 93922
800-333-3510
www.NGSP.com

Printed in the United States of America

ISBN 10: 0-7362-3551-5
ISBN 13: 978-0-7362-3551-8

10 11 12 13 14 15 9 8 7 6

Contents

Contents, *continued*

UNIT 4

UNIT 5

Contents, *continued*

Grammar: Adverbs

✔ Edit and Proofread

UNIT 6

Grammar: Sentence Variety

Grammar: Compound Sentences

Grammar: Complex Sentences

✔ Edit and Proofread

UNIT 7

Grammar: Present Perfect Tense

Grammar: Perfect Tenses

Grammar: Participles and Participial Phrases

Proofreader's Marks

Mark	Meaning	Example
≡	Capitalize.	I love new york city.
/	Do not capitalize.	I'm going shopping at my favorite Store.
⊙	Add a period.	Mr⊙Lopez is our neighbor.
?	Add a question mark.	Where is my black pen?
↓	Add an exclamation point.	Look out↓
ᵛ ᵛ	Add quotation marks.	"You are late," said the teacher.
∧	Add a comma.	Amy∧how are you feeling today?
∧	Add a semicolon.	This shirt is nice∧however, that one brings out the color of your eyes.
◇	Add a colon.	He wakes up at 6◇30 a.m.
⊼	Add a dash.	Barney⊼he's my pet dog⊼has run away.
{}	Add parentheses.	I want to work for the Federal Bureau of Investigation{FBI}.
=	Add a hyphen.	You were born in mid=September, right?
ᵛ	Add an apostrophe.	Iᵛm the oldest of five children.
#	Add a space.	She likes him a#lot.
⌒	Close up a space.	How much home⌒work do you have?
∧	Add text.	My keys are ᵒⁿ∧the table.
ℯ	Delete.	I am going tooℯmy friend's house.
∧ℯ	Change text.	We have ᵗᵒᵒ∧ℯmuch garbage.
∩	Transpose words, letters.	Did you see th∩eir new car?
⑤ᵖ	Spell out.	Today he is turning ⑯ ⑤ᵖ
¶	Begin a new paragraph.	"I win!" I shouted.¶"No, you don't," he said.
ⓘtal__	Add italics.	The Spanish word for table is mesa. ⓘtal
ⓤ/ₛ__	Add underlining.	Little Women is one of my favorite books.

1 Are All Sentences the Same?

No. They Have Different Purposes.

Four Kinds of Sentences

1. Make a **statement** to tell something. End with a period.
   I can't decide what to do about my friend Bernie.

2. Ask a **question** to find out something. End with a question mark.
   Would you like to talk about it?

3. Use an **exclamation** to express a strong feeling. End with an exclamation point.
   Yes, I need help!

4. Give a **command** to tell someone what to do. End with a period.
   Stop worrying. Tell me about it. Don't leave anything out.

Start every sentence with a capital letter.

Try It

A. Read each sentence. Decide what kind of sentence it is. Write **statement**, **question**, **exclamation**, or **command** on the line.

1. What did Bernie do? _____question_____

2. I think he cheated on the math test. _____statement_____

3. Don't tell anyone. _____command_____

4. I can't believe it! _____exclamation_____

B. Change each sentence to the kind in parentheses. Use correct punctuation.

Possible responses:

5. I saw Bernie get the answers from another student. **(question)** _Did you see Bernie get the answers from another student?_

6. Did you tell Mrs. Lynch about it? **(command)** _Tell Mrs. Lynch about it._

Write It

C. Answer the questions about a difficult choice you have made. Use at least two different kinds of sentences in your responses. Use correct punctuation.

7. What kind of choice did you make? I had to choose _____

_____.

8. Why was it difficult to make your choice? _____

_____

9. Did anyone help you make that choice? _____

_____

D. (10–14) Write at least five sentences to tell more about your choice. Vary the kinds of sentences in your response.

_____

_____

_____

_____

_____

Edit It

E. (15–20) Edit the journal entry. Fix the six mistakes. The first is done for you. Make sure to use correct punctuation for each kind of sentence.

December 10

I don't think our school does enough recycling.

I don't like that the cafeteria uses foam cups.

Why don't they use paper cups and plates?

I want to help the environment. I'm just so

frustrated! Should I complain to the principal?

Proofreader's Marks
Add a period:
I am happy with my choices.
Add an exclamation point:
What a tough decision!
Add a question mark:
How did you make your choice?
See all Proofreader's Marks on page ix.

2

② What Do You Need for a Sentence?

A Subject and a Predicate

A complete sentence has two parts: the **subject** and the **predicate**.

subject   predicate

Kim plays baseball.

To find the parts, in most sentences, ask yourself:

1. Whom or what is the sentence about? Your answer is the **subject**.

2. What does the subject do? Your answer is the **predicate**.

Sentence	Whom or What?	What Does the Subject Do?
I joined the team.	I	joined the team
The coach gives me advice.	The coach	gives me advice

Try It

A. Match each subject with a predicate to make a complete sentence.

1. Our team ———————————— is one of the best teams around.

2. Mr. Harrison ⟋ try to beat us.

3. All of his players ⟍ coaches our team well.

4. He ———————— asks us to do our best.

5. Other teams work hard during practice.

6. The crowds win lots of games!

7. We cheer when we play.

8. Total commitment ———————— is necessary on our team.

B. Choose a subject and a predicate from each column to make four sentences. Write the sentences on the lines. Use the words only once. Sentences will vary.

Subject	Predicate
One player	makes practice a priority now.
Coach Harrison	gave Harry one more chance.
The team	agreed with that decision.
Harry	missed practice often.

9. _One player missed practice often._

10. _Coach Harrison gave Harry one more chance._

11. _The team agreed with that decision._

12. _Harry makes practice a priority now._

Write It

C. Imagine your best friend is on a rival baseball team. When your team plays against his team, what do you do? Make sure you use a subject and a predicate in each sentence.

13. Do you hope he makes mistakes so your team can win? I hope he _____
_____.

14. Is it hard to play against your friend? Why or why not? _____
_____

15. How do you think your friend feels about the issue? _____
_____

D. (16–20) Write at least five sentences to tell more about how you would handle the situation. Use subjects and predicates correctly.

_____
_____
_____
_____
_____

4

③ What Is a Sentence About?
The Subject

The **complete subject** can be one word or several words. Zoom in on the most important word. Is it a noun? A **noun** is the name of a person, place, thing, or idea.

1. My **neighborhood** had trouble with telephone service last night.
2. A **storm** damaged the telephone lines.
3. The **wind** knocked down some trees.
4. My **friend** tried to call me.
5. **Liz** didn't know the phone didn't work.
6. "The **problem** was the phone," I explained to her.

Nouns in the Subject	
Person	friend
	Liz
Place	neighborhood
Thing	storm
	wind
Idea	problem

Try It

A. Add a noun to complete the subject of the sentence.   Possible responses:

1–2. My best ____friend____ lives next door. His ____name____ is Sidney.

3. Our funniest ____memory____ includes the day we met.

4. His ____family____ moved to our neighborhood last year.

5. My ____mother____ decided to bake them cookies.

B. Complete each sentence with a subject. Use the type of noun in parentheses.
Possible responses:

6. ____I____ offered to bring them the cookies. **(person)**

7. The ____plate____ slipped out of my hand. **(thing)**

8. Their ____yard____ was covered with cookies. **(place)**

9. The ____situation____ made us laugh so hard our stomachs hurt! **(idea)**

Write It

C. Answer the questions about a good friend. Make sure each sentence has a subject.

10. Is your friend an old or a new friend? _____

11. How did you meet? _____

12. What do you like best about your friend? _____

_____

13. What do you think your friend likes about you? _____

_____

14. Does your friend ever help you? How? _____

_____

D. (15–19) Write at least five sentences to tell about things you and your friend enjoy doing together.

_____

_____

_____

_____

_____

Edit It

E. (20–25) Edit the article to include a complete subject. Fix the six mistakes.
Possible responses:

Making Friends

Many students have trouble making friends. These tips can help ease
the process. Look for people with similar interests. A class at school is a
good start. Do you like music? Sign up for chorus or band class.
You can conquer your shyness. Shake hands and say hello. A new friend is
worth the effort!

Proofreader's Marks

Add text:

friends
New are fun.

See all Proofreader's Marks
on page ix.

4 What's the Most Important Word in the Predicate?

The Verb

- The **complete predicate** in a sentence often tells what the subject does. The **verb** shows the action.

  We **talk** about the school election.

  We **vote** for our favorite candidate.

- Sometimes the predicate tells what the subject has. It uses these **verbs**:

  I **have** a friend named Janice.

  She **has** a good chance of winning.

- Other times, the predicate tells what the subject is or is like. The **verb** is a form of **be**.

  The school election **is** next week.

  We **are** great supporters of Janice.

  I **am** on the election committee.

Try It

A. Complete each sentence with a verb. Possible responses:

1. Our school _____needs_____ a president.

2. Every year we _____vote_____ for a new president.

3. I think Janice _____is_____ a fine candidate.

4. Tim _____tells_____ everyone about Janice.

5. Janice _____has_____ many friends at school.

6. Her friends _____are_____ impressed with her.

7. I _____hope_____ she wins.

8. Even Ben _____thinks_____ her name belongs on the ballot.

B. Choose words from each column to build five sentences about school elections. You can use words more than once. Possible responses:

Janice We Tim and Ben	is are need want	her to win. a good candidate. volunteers. a good school president.

9. _Janice is a good candidate._

10. _Tim and Ben are volunteers._

11. _We need a good school president._

12. _We want her to win._

13. _Tim and Ben want a good school president._

Write It

C. Answer the questions about school elections. Use verbs correctly.

14. Do your classmates get involved in school elections? _____

_____

15. What makes someone a good school president? _____

_____

D. (16–20) Write at least five sentences to tell why you would be a good school president. Use verbs correctly.

_____

_____

_____

_____

_____

5 Write Complete Sentences

Remember: You need a **subject** and a **predicate** to make a complete sentence. Often, the most important word in the subject is a **noun**. Every predicate needs a **verb**.

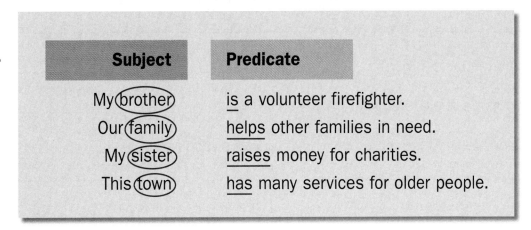

Subject	Predicate
My (brother)	<u>is</u> a volunteer firefighter.
Our (family)	<u>helps</u> other families in need.
My (sister)	<u>raises</u> money for charities.
This (town)	<u>has</u> many services for older people.

Try It

A. Add a subject or a predicate to complete each sentence. Possible responses:

1. Sometimes _____people_____ need a helping hand.

2. _____Betty_____ works at a homeless shelter.

3. _____She_____ encourages me to help others.

4. I _____decide_____ she is right.

5. I _____think_____ I will volunteer, too.

6. The hospital _____is_____ a good place to volunteer.

B. Circle the noun or pronoun in the subject and underline the verb in the predicate in each sentence.

7. My (parents) <u>set</u> a good example for me.

8. Their (choices) <u>are</u> usually logical.

9. (I) <u>follow</u> their example.

10. My (family) <u>talks</u> about a choice I made.

C. Answer the questions about how you make decisions. Use complete sentences.

11. How do family members help you make decisions? Sometimes _____ help

_____.

12. Who gives you the best advice? _____

13. Do you make some choices on your own? _____

14. Do you consider all the facts carefully when you make a decision? _____

_____

D. (15–18) Write at least four sentences to tell about how you make good decisions. Make sure each sentence includes both a subject and a predicate.

_____

_____

_____

_____

_____

Edit It

E. (19–25) Edit the list. Fix the seven mistakes to make complete sentences.

Possible responses:

Rules to Live By

1. I always use good judgment.
2. I make decisions logically.
3. First, I think carefully about the facts.
4. Second, I think about the consequences.
5. Then I talk to people I trust.
6. I listen to what others say.
7. Finally, I do what I believe is right.
8. That is the best I can do.

Proofreader's Marks
Add text:
I always think carefully.
See all Proofreader's Marks on page ix.

6 What's a Plural Noun?

A Word That Names More Than One Thing

One	More Than One
A **singular noun** names one thing.	A **plural noun** names more than one thing.

Use these spelling rules for forming plural nouns.

1. To make most nouns plural, just add **-s**.

2. If the noun ends in **s**, **z**, **sh**, **ch**, or **x**, add **-es**.

3. If the noun ends in **y** after the consonant, change the **y** to **i** and add **-es**.

4. Some nouns have special plural forms.

One	More Than One
choice	choic**es**
box	box**es**
family	famil**ies**
child	children
person	people

Try It

A. (1–4) Read these nouns: **classes, fly, plans, dish**. Which nouns are singular and which are plural? Put each noun in the correct column. Then add its other form. The first one is done for you.

Singular Nouns (one)		Plural Nouns (more than one)	
class	fly	classes	flies
plan	dish	plans	dishes

B. Write the plural form of the singular noun in parentheses.

5. Some ____children____ are influenced by their peers. **(child)**

6. They do not make ____decisions____ on their own. **(decision)**

7. To be accepted, they might do things that go against their true ____wishes____. **(wish)**

Write It

C. Answer the questions about who or what influences your choices.
Use singular and plural nouns in your response.

8. Who influences your decisions the most? I am influenced the most by _____

_____.

9. Do you feel pressure to be like other students? _____

10. Are you influenced by outside sources, like people you see on television or in the movies?

_____

_____

D. (11–14) Write at least four sentences to tell more about who or what influences your
choices. Use at least two singular nouns and two plural nouns in your response.

_____

_____

_____

_____

Edit It

E. (15–20) Edit the journal entry. Fix the six mistakes. Make sure you use the
correct noun form for each sentence.

February 16

I am determined to make my own decisions.
Certain studentes ^ *students* at my school try to
convince other peoples ^ *people* to make poor choice ^ *choices*.
They encourage them to smoke or drink.
Sometimes I even see very young childrens ^ *children*
with cigarettes. These boies ^ *boys* and girls do not
really want to smoke. They just go along
with the crowd to be popular. I wish more
person ^ *people* would think for themselves!

Proofreader's Marks

Change text: *children*
Many ~~child~~ are not so
lucky. ^

See all Proofreader's Marks
on page ix.

7 How Do You Know What Verb to Use?

Match It to the Subject.

- Use **I** with **am**.

  I am in the school auditorium.

- Use **he**, **she**, or **it** with **is**.

  It is filled with students. A guest **speaker is** on stage.

  He is a professional athlete.

- Use **we**, **you**, or **they** with **are**.

  My **friends are** athletes, too. **They are** fans of the speaker.

  We are curious about his life. **Are you**?

Forms of *Be*
I **am**
he, she, or it **is**
we, you, or they **are**

Try It

A. Complete each sentence about a role model. Use **am**, **is**, or **are**.

1. The guest speaker _____is_____ from my neighborhood.

2. He _____is_____ able to inspire teens. He uses his life story as an example.

3. He knows it _____is_____ not easy to study, work, and play sports.

4. "Coaches and teachers can help," he says. "They _____are_____ on your side."

5. I _____am_____ confident that I can achieve my dream with hard work.

B. (6–11) Read the interview. Write **am**, **is**, or **are** on each line.

Q. Who _____is_____ your role model?

A. My dad _____is_____ my role model. I _____am_____ proud of how hard he works. He _____is_____ now a business owner. My mom shares the responsibilities. They _____are_____ happy about the business.

Q. Describe one trait that you and your dad share. How are you the same?

A. We _____are_____ both impatient! We always try to finish things quickly.

C. Answer the questions about yourself and your role model.

12. What are your talents? I _____ *good at* _____.

13. What is one goal you have? *My goal* _____ *to* _____.

14. Who is your role model? _____

15. How is this person a good role model? _____

_____

D. (16–19) Write at least four sentences to tell more about yourself and your role model.

_____

_____

_____

_____

_____

Edit It

E. (20–25) Edit the journal entry. Fix the six mistakes.

March 31

I think hard work is the best way to achieve
my goal. My dreams is big. I are dedicated.
(are) *(am)* *(are)*
My friends is not always as serious. They is
(are) *(are)*
not worried about money, college, or jobs.
However, I choose to work and study. My
family am helpful. Together, we be a team.
(is) *(are)*
My sister is a good example. She is a success
already.

Proofreader's Marks

Change text:
are
We is successful.
∧

See all Proofreader's Marks
on page ix.

14

8 How Do You Know What Action Verb to Use?

Match It to the Subject.

- **Action verbs** tell when a subject does something, like **ride**, **look**, or **drive**. If the sentence is about one other person, place, or thing, add **-s** to the action verb.

  1. My sisters **ride** the bus.   **2.** Our cousin **rides** the bus, too.

  3. We **look** out the window.   **4.** A driver **looks** at us.

  5. My parents **drive** the car.   **6.** Dad **drives** us to the store.

- If there is more than one action verb in a sentence, all verbs must agree with the subject:

  My neighbor **drives**, **parks**, and **locks** his car.

Try It

A. Complete each sentence about money. Write the correct verb.

1. My parents _____*give*_____ me money for lunch at school.
give / gives

2. I _____need_____ to earn my own spending money.
need / needs

3. My sisters _____work_____ after school.
work / works

4. I _____find_____ many reasons for spending money.
find / finds

5. I _____save_____ a little money each week.
save / saves

6. My mom _____asks_____ me to save for an emergency or for a vacation.
ask / asks

7. I _____work_____ on the weekends.
work / works

8. My friends call me, _____ask_____ to go out, and forget that I need money.
ask / asks

9. I decide to stay home. My sister _____stays_____ home with me.
stay / stays

B. Choose words from each column to build six sentences about getting a ride to school. You can use words more than once.

Teresa She I	asks owns want ask work	an extra shift. a car. for gas money. for a ride.

10. _____

11. _____

12. _____

13. _____

14. _____

15. _____

Write It

C. Your friend at work adds extra hours to her timesheet. You want to earn more money, too. Do you add more hours to your timesheet, or do you tell the store owner?

16. Do you think adding extra time is right? I _____

_____.

17. How does your friend cause a problem for you? She _____

_____

_____.

D. (18–20) Write at least three sentences to tell more about your choice. Use action verbs correctly.

_____

_____

_____

_____

⑨ What's a Compound Subject?

It's a Subject with Two or More Nouns.

When a subject has two or more nouns joined by **and** or **or**, it is called a **compound subject**.

1. **Adults and children** help our community.
2. **Henry and Fiona** plan a fundraiser.
3. A **book sale or** a **cake sale** makes money.
4. The **parents or** the **school** needs to help.
5. The **school or** the **parents** need to help.

How do you know what verb to use with a compound subject?

- If you see **and**, use a plural verb like **help** or **plan**.
- If you see **or**, look at the last noun in the subject. Is it singular? Then use a singular verb. Is it plural? Then use a plural verb.

Try It

A. Write the correct form of the verb in parentheses.

1. My classmates and our community _____ work _____ together to make

      work / works
   our town beautiful.

2. The bank and the grocery store _____ donate _____ money for a new park.

      donate / donates

3. Parents and teens _____ plant _____ trees.

      plant / plants

4. The mayor and police officers _____ help _____, too.

      help / helps

5. An adult or teens _____ bring _____ shovels.

      bring / brings

6. My friends and my classmates _____ water _____ the new plants.

      water / waters

7. The parents or the school _____ takes _____ photos.

      take / takes

B. Complete each sentence with a compound subject to match the verb. Possible responses:

8. ___Jason___ and ___Margaret___ volunteer at the local hospital.

9. My ___brother___ and my ___sister___ volunteer there, too.

10. The ___nurses___ and the ___patients___ keep my brother and sister busy.

11. Both ___children___ and ___adults___ love to see them.

12. ___Jason___ or ___Margaret___ visits every Saturday.

Write It

C. Answer the questions about community service. Use compound subjects correctly.

13. What do you do to help at home or at school? _____

_____

14. What accomplishments are you proud of? _____

_____

_____

15. Which two places in your community would you most like to volunteer? _____

_____

_____

D. (16–20) Write at least five sentences to tell why you would choose to do community service. Make sure you use at least two compound subjects.

_____

_____

_____

_____

_____

_____

⑩ Make Subjects and Verbs Agree

Remember: The verb you use depends on your subject. These subjects and verbs go together:

Forms of *Be*	Action Verbs
I **am** interested.	I **join** the club.
You **are** interested.	You **join** the club, too.
He, she, or it **is** interested.	He, she, or it **joins** the club.
We, you, or they **are** interested.	We, you, or they **join** the club.
My friends **are** interested.	Teenagers **join** the club.
My friends and I **are** interested.	My friends and I **join** the club.

Try It

A. Complete each sentence about careers. Write the verb that goes with the subject.

1. My friend Ana and I _____ join _____ the career club.
   join / joins

2. Ana _____ wants _____ to study business.
   want / wants

3. She _____ is _____ interested in marketing.
   is / are

4. I _____ am _____ interested in a career in health.
   is / am

5. I also _____ want _____ to study large animals.
   want / wants

B. Write the correct form of the verb in parentheses.

6. John and Bianca _____ read _____ about careers at the library. **(read)**

7. John _____ hopes _____ to be a pilot. **(hope)**

8. He _____ meets _____ a pilot on career day. **(meet)**

9. John _____ talks _____ to the pilot about his career choice. **(talk)**

C. Answer the questions about your future career. Make sure your subjects and verbs agree.

10. What careers are you interested in? I _____ interested in _____

_____.

11. Do you know anyone who works in one of these careers? What do they do? _____

_____

12. What would you like to ask them about their career? I _____

_____.

D. (13–15) Write at least three sentences to tell more about a career you would like to choose. Make sure each verb agrees with its subject.

_____

_____

_____

_____

Edit It

E. (16–20) Edit the letter. Fix the five mistakes with verbs.

Dear Aunt Dorothy,

I think about my future a lot these days. Yesterday, we had Career Day at school. Now I has lots of information [have] about different careers. I met a research scientist. She are very excited about her job. She make important [is] [makes] decisions every day. I am interested in a career in science. I are also quite interested in a career in music. That is [am] why I am writing to you. Do you like your career? Is you [Are] happy as a professional guitarist?

Love,

Marina

Proofreader's Marks
Change text:
She ~~are~~ successful. [is]
See all Proofreader's Marks on page ix.

⑪ What Is a Fragment?

It's an Incomplete Sentence.

A **fragment** is a group of words that begins with a capital letter and ends with a period. It looks like a sentence, but it is not complete. A subject or a verb may be missing.

Fragments	Sentences
1. Moves to a new town.	Tina moves to a new town.
2. She the school.	She likes the school.
3. The teens in the park.	The teens meet in the park.
4. Makes new friends.	She makes new friends.

Try It

A. Write whether each group of words is a fragment or a sentence. If it is a fragment, add a subject or a verb. Write the complete sentence. Possible responses:

1. Jason to a new school. _fragment; Jason goes to a new school._ _____

_____

2. Students at the new school study hard. __sentence_____

_____

3. Decides to study harder this year. __fragment; Jason decides to study harder____
   __this year._____

B. (4–8) Each group of words in the paragraph is a fragment. Add a subject or a verb to complete each sentence. Possible responses:

Everyone _____plays_____ sports at my new school. All of the students

_____want_____ to play on a team. My old _____school_____ was different. Most

_____students_____ there did not play sports. I _____am_____ glad to be here

because I love sports!

C. Answer the questions about your school. Use complete sentences in your response.

9. What do you like best about your school? My favorite _____

_____.

10. Do you and your classmates share many of the same interests? _____

_____

11. Do you think a new student would feel welcome at your school? Why or why not? _____

_____

D. (12–14) Write at least three sentences that would give a new student a good idea of what your school is like. Read your sentences aloud. Fix any fragments you might hear.

_____

_____

_____

_____

_____

Edit It

E. (15–20) Edit the letter. Fix the six fragments. Add a subject or a verb. Possible responses:

Dear Samantha,

You are on my mind today. I miss seeing you at school. This school is different from our school back in Oklahoma. The classes here are very full and noisy. I try to fit in. It is not always easy. A student is helping me. Her name is Clarisse. She encourages me to join the chorus. I like to sing. I guess it is good to try new things!

Your friend,

Marion

Proofreader's Marks

Add text:
make
They ^ friends easily.

See all Proofreader's Marks on page ix.

12 What's One Way to Fix a Fragment?

Add a Subject.

- A complete sentence has a **subject** and a **predicate**.
- To check for a subject, ask yourself:
  Whom or what is the sentence about?

Fragments	Sentences
1. Reads a magazine.	**Charlene** reads a magazine.
2. Sees a picture of a dress she likes.	**She** sees a picture of a dress she likes.
3. Buys the dress.	**She** buys the dress.
4. Says Charlene looks like a movie star.	**Maya** says Charlene looks like a movie star.

Try It

A. (1–5) Fix the five fragments. Add a subject to make a complete sentence.

Premiere Soap Promises a Flawless Complexion
Premiere Soap is used by real TV stars. It Makes your skin feel as
soft as silk. Many people across the nation buy it. They See amazing
results. They Find that their skin improves within days. Actress Sadie
Chanelle uses Premiere Soap. She Has a flawless complexion. You Can, too!
Try our soap for five days. You will see results.

Proofreader's Marks

Do not capitalize:

The Actress is talented.

Add text:
are
Movies exciting.

See all Proofreader's Marks on page ix.

B. (6–10) Draw a line from each subject to the correct predicate.   Possible responses:

6. I ——————————————— saw a new product on television.

7. It ———————— buy those sneakers.

8. All my friends ———————— think the sneakers look cool.

9. They ———————— is a pair of sneakers that light up.

10. My brother ——————— says he thinks they look stupid.

Write It

C. Answer the questions about the influence of TV, movies, and magazines on you and your peers. Make sure each sentence has a subject.

11. Are you influenced by the behavior of famous actors? I _____

_____.

12. Do you buy certain products because they are advertised on television? _____

_____

13. Which celebrity do you admire the most? _____

_____

14. What qualities do you admire in this person? _____

_____

15. Are many of your friends influenced by celebrities? How? _____

_____

D. (16–20) Write at least five sentences. Tell how your choices and actions are influenced by specific people you read about in magazines or see on television or in movies. Then read your sentences aloud. Fix any fragments.

_____

_____

_____

_____

_____

_____

13 What's Another Way to Fix a Fragment?

Add a Predicate, and Be Sure It Has a Verb.

When you write a sentence, be sure to include the verb. If you leave out the verb, the words you wrote are a **fragment**. Study the sentences in the chart.

Fragments	Sentences
1. Josh his older brother.	Josh **admires** his older brother.
2. He the Best Track Athlete award.	He **won** the Best Track Athlete award.
3. Josh a medal, too.	Josh **wants** a medal, too.
4. He each morning.	He **runs** each morning.

Try It

A. (1–5) Fix the five fragments. Add a verb to make a complete sentence.

July 5

My friend Ben creates beautiful paintings. He ^is^
a terrific artist. I ^want^ to learn to paint, too. Ben ^says^
he will teach me. I ^am^ eager to get started on
a picture. I ^think^ my dog King should be my first
model!

Proofreader's Marks

Add text: have
Artists ^ fun.

See all Proofreader's Marks on page ix.

B. Complete each sentence with a verb. Possible responses:

6. Harry ____plays____ the piano.

7. Harry's brother ____is____ a concert pianist.

8. Harry ____works____ hard at his lessons.

9. He ____wants____ to play as well as his brother.

C. Think about friends and family that you admire. Have their successes influenced the way you think about your own personal goals? Write complete sentences.

10. Who do you admire? I admire _____

_____ .

11. How has their example influenced your own personal goals? _____

_____

_____

D. (12–15) Write at least four sentences to tell more about your personal goals. Then read your sentences aloud. Fix any fragments you might hear.

_____

_____

_____

_____

_____

_____

Edit It

E. (16–20) Edit the journal entry below. Fix the five fragments. Add a verb to form a complete sentence.

Proofreader's Marks

Add text:
likes
Louise ∧ math.

April 22

I am very happy with my project. I ∧ a weekly
                                    have
study group at my house. It ∧ like the one
                            is
Uncle Charlie used to have. My friends and
I ∧ better grades now. Each group member
get
∧ in charge of one subject. I ∧ sure everyone
is   make
understands math.

26

⑭ What's One More Way to Fix a Fragment?

Combine Neighboring Sentences.

Writers may create a fragment by starting a new sentence when they shouldn't. These fragments are easy to fix. Just combine the fragment with the sentence before it.

    ┌───── sentence ─────┐ ┌──── fragment ────┐

1. Irina used to set the table. While her father cooked dinner.

Irina used to set the table while her father cooked dinner.

    ┌──── sentence ────┐ ┌──── fragment ────┐

2. Now Irina cooks dinner. Because her father is busy.

Now Irina cooks dinner because her father is busy.

Try It

A. Find each fragment. Combine it with the other sentence and write the new sentence.

1. Irina's sister is a role model for her. Because she is so intelligent. _Irina's sister is a role model for her because she is so intelligent._

2. Irina wanted to be a nurse like her sister. When she was younger. _Irina wanted to be a nurse like her sister when she was younger._

3. Now she has other ideas. Because she learned about more careers. _Now she has other ideas because she learned about more careers._

4. She learned about new careers. When she attended Career Day at school. _She learned about new careers when she attended Career Day at school._

5. She is considering a career in law. Or studying finance. _She is considering a career in law or studying finance._

6. Her father is a lawyer. And works at a law firm. _Her father is a lawyer and works at a law firm._

B. Rewrite each sentence by adding a fragment from the box. Punctuate your sentences correctly.

Because her interests have changed.	And speaks Spanish.
Who is a teacher.	Because his brother is one.

7. John wants to be an electrician. _John wants to be an electrician because his brother is one._

8. Gretchen is influenced by her sister. _Gretchen is influenced by her sister who is a teacher._

9. Kate's mother is from Ecuador. _Kate's mother is from Ecuador and speaks Spanish._

10. Tina doesn't know what to do. _Tina doesn't know what to do because her interests have changed._

Write It

C. Complete each sentence with your own ideas and beliefs about how you and your interests have changed over time. Use complete sentences.

11. I used to enjoy _____.

12. I was interested in that because _____.

13. Now I prefer to _____.

14. My interest changed because _____.

15. Another way I have changed is _____.

D. (16–20) Write at least five sentences to tell more about how you and your interests have changed. Then read your sentences aloud. Fix any fragments.

_____

_____

_____

_____

_____

28

15 Fix Sentence Fragments

Remember: You can fix a fragment by adding a subject or predicate that includes a verb. Or, you can combine the fragment with another sentence.

Fragment:	Tells Ella about the race.
Sentence:	Bonnie tells Ella about the race.
Fragment:	Bonnie Ella to try to win.
Sentence:	Bonnie wants Ella to try to win.
Fragment:	Ella is not sure. If she wants to enter the race.
Sentence:	Ella is not sure if she wants to enter the race.

Try It

A. Fix the fragments and write complete sentences. Possible responses:

1. Is a big influence on Juan. _Kevin is a big influence on Juan._

2. Juan. _Juan admires Kevin._

3. Juan listens carefully to Kevin. Because he has good ideas. _Juan listens carefully to Kevin because he has good ideas._

4. Thinks things over, but he makes his own decisions. _He thinks things over, but he makes his own decisions._

B. Each group of words is a fragment. Add a subject or a verb or combine the fragment with the other sentence. Write the complete sentence. Possible responses:

5. Had to make a choice. _I had to make a choice._

6. David me advice. _David gave me advice._

7. Had a similar experience. _He had a similar experience._

8. His comments were helpful. Because he has a lot of experience. _His comments were helpful because he has a lot of experience._

Write It

C. Answer the questions about a decision you have made. Make sure your sentences are complete. Include a subject and a predicate with a verb.

9. What was a big decision you have made? I decided to _____

_____.

10. What advice did you get? _____

_____

11. Did you do what they suggested? Why or why not? _____

_____

D. (12–15) Write at least four sentences to tell more about your decision. What other influences did you consider when you made your decision? Then read your sentences aloud. Fix any fragments.

_____

_____

_____

_____

_____

Edit It

E. (16–20) Edit the advice letter. Fix five mistakes.

Dear Chris,

    I am glad you asked for my advice about your friend. You Have
a difficult decision to make. Think you should tell your friend
the truth. A good friendship is based on honesty. And honesty
is so important. That is just my opinion. You have to decide.
What seems right to you.

Your cousin,

Andy

Proofreader's Marks
Delete:
I know what to do now.
Do not capitalize:
They Told me.
Add text: is
It my idea.
See all Proofreader's Marks on page ix.

30

✓ Capitalize Proper Nouns and Adjectives

Proper nouns are capitalized because they name specific people, places, and things. Common nouns, which are general, are not capitalized.

Common Noun	Proper Noun
principal	Principal Edwards
state	Florida

Proper adjectives, which come from proper nouns, are also capitalized.

Proper Noun	Proper Adjective
Japan	Japanese
Boston	Bostonian

Try It

A. Use proofreader's marks to correct the capitalization error in each sentence.

1. My mom and I went to our favorite italian restaurant to talk about our big move.

2. We had to decide which City we would move to, Chicago or Miami.

3. I had never been to Chicago, but I had been to illinois.

4. I decided to look at a map of the United states.

Proofreader's Marks

Capitalize:

My mother is from japan.

Do not capitalize:

I like Japanese Food.

See all Proofreader's Marks on page ix.

B. (5–11) Edit the journal entry. Fix the seven mistakes. The first is done for you.

My mom suggested I do more research about each City. I looked in a miami Newspaper. There was an article about a new Art school. It is the best one in the State. They have special programs in latin music and asian art.

✔ Punctuate Quotations Correctly

- Use quotation marks (" ") around the exact words that people speak. Do not use quotation marks when you describe what people said.

   Quotation: "I made my choice," I said to my mom.

   Description: I told my mom that I made my choice.

- Use a comma to set off **tags**, or words that identify who is quoted.

   She replied, "I'm glad that you made your choice."

   "I'm glad that you made your choice," **she replied**.

   "I'm glad," **she replied,** "that you made your choice."

Try It

A. Edit each sentence. Add or delete quotation marks and commas.

12. She said that we didn't have to move if I didn't want to."

13. I replied "I'm ready for a fresh start."

14. "A fresh start" she said, "would be good for both of us."

15. I told my mom "everything I found out about each city.

16. Then I said, "Miami has a new art school."

17. My mom asked, "Is it expensive?"

18. I replied "Maybe I can get a scholarship."

19. She said, "That would be perfect."

Proofreader's Marks

Add quotation marks:
   My mom said, "Pick the city that will make you happy."

Add comma:
   "Thank you," I replied.

Delete:
   She said we could go.

B. Rewrite the following descriptive sentences so that they include quotations. Possible responses:

20. My mom told me to send in my application. ___My mom said, "Send in your application."___

21. I told her I sent it in yesterday. ___I said, "I sent it in yesterday."___

✓ Check Your Spelling

Homonyms are words that sound alike but have different meanings and spellings. Spell these homonyms correctly when you proofread.

Homonyms and Their Meanings	Examples
it's (contraction) = it is; it has	**It's** scary to apply to a new school.
its (adjective) = belonging to it	The school made **its** decision.
there (adverb) = that place or position	I got accepted. I'm going **there**.
their (adjective) = belonging to them	The teachers like **their** new theater.
they're (contraction) = they are	**They're** happy to have a new student.

Try It

A. Use proofreader's marks to correct the homonym errors.

22. Our neighbors are moving, too. ~~Their~~ They're moving to Boston.

23. ~~There~~ Their new house is bigger than the one they live in now.

24. We are going ~~their~~ there to visit them in the fall.

25. ~~Its~~ It's beautiful in the city at that time of the year.

26. The city has ~~it's~~ its apple festival in the fall.

Proofreader's Marks

Change text:
There
~~Their~~ are two cities we like.

B. (27–32) Complete the story. Add a correct homonym to each sentence.

I was excited about the art school, and I immediately began to fantasize about going _____there_____. _____It's_____ the best art school in the state. I read more about the school online. _____Their_____ theater program includes field trips to Broadway plays. _____They're_____ accepting applications now for next year. The school sends _____its_____ response in June. _____It's_____ so hard to wait!

✔ Check Sentences for Completeness

A sentence is complete when it expresses a complete thought and has two parts: the **subject** and the **predicate**. A **subject** tells who. A **predicate** tells what the subject does. Every predicate needs a **verb**.

Problem	Solution
1. Sentence is missing a subject. Received a promotion.	**Add the missing subject.** She received a promotion.
2. Sentence is missing a verb. Her boss happy with her work.	**Add the missing verb.** Her boss was happy with her work.
3. Fragments are not sentences. He wanted her to open a new branch office. In Miami.	**Join the fragments.** He wanted her to open a new branch office in Miami.

Try It

A. Match each subject to the correct predicate to form a complete sentence.

33. My mom and I   gave her a promotion.

34. Then she   ate at our favorite restaurant.

35. Her boss   were opening a new office in Miami.

36. The company   was expanding.

37. They   told me the big news.

B. (38–40) Edit the journal entry. Fix the three incomplete sentences.

Proofreader's Marks

Delete text and do not capitalize:

I gave her The full presentation.

Add text:
                was
Mom ⌃ glad about her promotion.

January 23

She told me we didn't have to move if I didn't want to. I wasn't sure if I wanted. To move or not. Went online to find out more about Miami. This was not an easy decision.

16 Is the Subject of a Sentence Always a Noun?

No, It Can Be a Pronoun.

- Use **I** when you talk about yourself.

  I love to paint. **I** want to take classes to learn more about it.

- Use **you** when you talk to another person.

  You learned to play the drums at a very young age.

- Use **he** when you talk about one man or one boy.

  My father is a comic book artist. **He** began drawing in high school.

- Use **she** when you talk about one woman or one girl.

  My aunt likes to write. **She** writes poems for a magazine.

- Use **it** when you talk about one place, thing, or idea.

  My brother wrote a song. **It** has a great rhythm.

Subject Pronouns
Singular
I
you
he, she, it

Try It

A. Complete each sentence. Use a subject pronoun from the chart.

1. Creativity can be developed through many activities. _____It_____ makes the world interesting and exciting.

2. Phillip is a wonderful writer. _____He_____ wrote an excellent story.

3. The story was about flying an airplane. _____It_____ was very exciting to read.

4. My favorite hobby is singing. _____I_____ sing almost every day.

5. Mayalinn painted a picture of a flying saucer. _____You_____ have to see it to believe it!

6. I told the artist, "_____You_____ are very talented."

7. My mother is creative. _____She_____ paints beautiful murals.

B. (8–14) Complete each sentence with a subject pronoun from the box.

She	He	It	I	You

My older sister Julia is a dancer. _____*She*_____ began dancing when she was five years old. My father saw that she had talent. _____*He*_____ signed Julia up for dance lessons. After high school, Julia went to a special institute for dancers. There, _____*she*_____ danced in shows. A man from a theater company saw one of the shows. _____*He*_____ asked my sister to join his theater. She accepted. Now Julia travels with many dancers across the country. Her job is demanding. _____*It*_____ requires a lot of hard work, but Julia loves it. I see several of her shows each year. _____*I*_____ am proud of my sister. _____*You*_____ would be impressed with her dancing, too.

Write It

C. Answer the questions about creative talents. Use complete sentences and subject pronouns.

15. What is your talent? _____ am talented at _____
_____.

16. Who helped you realize you had this talent? _____ helped me. _____
told me that _____.

17. What steps can you take to develop your talent? _____
_____
_____

D. (18–20) Write at least three sentences about creative people in your family. Use subject pronouns in your sentences.

_____
_____
_____
_____
_____
_____

17 Can a Pronoun Show "More Than One"?

Yes, It Can.

- Use **we** to talk about yourself and another person.

    My friends and I wrote a play.

    We will act it out on Friday.

- Use **you** to talk to one or more persons.

    You like our school plays, don't you?

    You should all be there on Friday.

- Use **they** to talk about more than one person or thing.

    Many other students helped us.

    They wanted to help tell the story.

Subject Pronouns	
Singular	**Plural**
I	we
you	you
he, she, it	they

Try It

A. Read the first sentence. Complete the second sentence with the correct subject pronoun.

1. My friends and I love acting. _____We_____ wrote a play.

2. Our play is about a boy named José. _____He_____ came from El Salvador at age seven.

3. His teachers notice that José has creative talent. _____They_____ praise his writing.

4. When José's mother reads his stories, _____she_____ knows that he will become a famous writer.

5. We will perform our play at school. _____It_____ will be a hit!

6. I would like you to go. _____You_____ should plan on attending.

7. You should bring your friends. _____They_____ will enjoy it.

8. I will send you an invitation. _____You_____ should respond by Friday.

B. Draw a line from the first sentence to the one that logically follows. Be sure the subject nouns and pronouns match.

9. My younger sister is very creative. — They admired her skills.

10. The art teacher got my sister involved in drawing for school. — We believe she can have a career as an artist.

11. Students saw her drawings and complimented her. — He asked her to draw a cartoon for the school paper.

12. My parents thought my sister could find more creative outlets. — They helped her find other ways to use her skills in the community.

13. The directors of a local day care wanted an artist to help paint murals on the walls. — She took an art class and found that she had talent for drawing and painting.

14. My parents and I suggested that my sister go to an art institute after high school. — They asked my sister to paint a picture in each room.

Write It

C. Answer the questions about a creative project you would like to participate in. Use subject pronouns where needed.

15. What creative project would you like to participate in? _____ would like to

_____ .

16. Whom would you like to work with? _____ would like to work with _____ .

17. What role would the other person have? _____ would help _____ .

18. Who would your audience be? _____

19. How would having a partner make a difference to the project? _____

D. (20–25) Write at least six sentences that tell more about what each person would bring to the project. Use subject pronouns.

_____

_____

_____

_____

_____

_____

18 Can a Compound Subject Include a Pronoun?

Yes, and the Pronoun Comes Last.

A **compound subject** can include nouns and pronouns joined by **and** or **or**.

1. **My brother and I** need an art studio. We ask our mother what to do.
2. **My father and she** suggest we fix up the attic.
3. **My brother and I** want to use the space for painting and sculpting.
4. **He and I** are very excited about the new room.
5. First, **our parents or we** need to clean out the attic.

How do you know where to place the pronoun?

- Nouns always come before pronouns.
- The pronoun **I** always comes last.

Try It

A. Complete each sentence. Write the correct compound subject.

1. _____*My brother and I*_____ have many ideas for our attic studio.
   I and my brother / My brother and I

2. _____*Our friends and we*_____ will make a list of things we need for the new room.
   We and our friends / Our friends and we

3. My friend Antonio has a truck. _____*My brother or he*_____ will pick up the truck.
   My brother or he / He or my brother

4. _____*My friend and I*_____ will check the carpet store for old scraps.
   I and my friend / My friend and I

B. (5-8) Complete each sentence about a project. Use compound subjects with a pronoun and the word and. *Possible responses:*

My parents decided to improve the backyard. My uncle _____*and they*_____ did most of the work. My uncle started right away. My father _____*and he*_____ removed the concrete walk. In its place, we decided to put small stones. My sister _____*and I*_____ did that. My sister wanted to plant flowers. My father _____*and she*_____ planted daisies.

Write It

C. Answer the questions about improving your bedroom. Use simple or compound subjects.

9. Why did you want to change your bedroom? _____ wanted to change my bedroom because _____.

10. What changes did you decide to make? _____ decided to _____
_____.

11. Who helped you? _____ helped me. _____ helped by _____
_____.

12. How did your changes improve your room? _____

D. (13–15) Write at least three sentences about a project you did with others to improve your home. Use simple and compound subjects.

_____

_____

_____

Edit It

E. (16–20) Edit the journal entry. Fix the five pronoun mistakes.

May 26

My friend Martha helped me decorate my room. I and Martha worked for hours. My parents and ~~us~~ we love the result! Martha's father gave me some shelves. I wonder how Martha and ~~him~~ he fit them into their car. The shelves look spectacular in my room. My brother or ~~me~~ I will take a photograph. Now my brother's friends and ~~are~~ he fixing his room.

Proofreader's Marks

Transpose words:
I and Bo painted my room.

Add text:
My brother and ⌃I hung posters. ⌃

Change text:
He or ~~me~~ I will take a photo. ⌃

See all Proofreader's Marks on page ix.

40

⑲ How Do You Avoid Confusion with Pronouns?

Match the Pronoun to the Noun.

If you're not sure which **pronoun** to use, first find the **noun** it goes with. Then ask yourself:

- Is the noun a man, a woman, or a thing?
  Use **he** for a man, **she** for a woman, and **it** for a thing.

- Is the noun singular or plural? If plural, use **we**, **you**, or **they**.

If a pronoun does not refer correctly to a noun, change the pronoun.

Incorrect: All of the **students** make pictures for the fundraiser. **He** work very hard.

Correct: All of the **students** make pictures for the fundraiser. **They** work very hard.

The pronouns in these sentences are correct. Do you know why?

1. **Students** need a new writing lab at school. **They** decide to have a fundraiser.

2. The **fundraiser** will be next week. **It** will be a carnival.

Try It

A. Complete the sentence with a pronoun that matches the underlined word or words.

1. The <u>students</u> in school play on old equipment. _____They_____ need new equipment.

2. <u>My classmates and I</u> want to help. _____We_____ ask to have a fundraiser.

3. We ask <u>Ms. Ruiz</u> for help. _____She_____ decides to ask the school board.

4. Ms. Ruiz describes our plan to the <u>members</u>. _____They_____ give us permission.

B. (5–8) Complete the sentences with correct pronouns. Possible responses:

Our class took a field trip to an art exhibit. _____We_____ loved the artwork. _____It_____ was a great trip. Thanh and Marie's favorite painting was of a little boy. _____They_____ thought it looked so lifelike. I am so glad that my classmates and I went to the museum. _____We_____ learned a lot about the art.

C. Answer the questions about an art event you attended. Use pronouns correctly.

9. What type of art event did you attend? _____ attended _____.

10. Who went with you? _____ and _____ went to the event.

11. Why did you go? _____

12. What did you do or see there? _____

13. How did you and your friends feel about the event? _____

_____

14. Would you recommend this event to others? Why or why not? _____

_____

D. (15–16) Write at least two sentences that tell more about this or another art event you attended. Use pronouns correctly.

_____

_____

_____

_____

Edit It

E. (17–20) Edit the letter. Fix the four mistakes in pronouns.

Dear Chelsey,

    I want to invite you to a music festival on Sunday. Would ~~she~~ *you* like to go with me? A few of our other friends are going, too. *We* ~~would~~ meet them there. Musicians from Honduras are playing. *They* ~~He~~ are bringing special instruments. If we get hungry, don't worry. ~~She~~ *We* can buy lunch at a food stand there. I hope you can go!

Your friend,

Chris

Proofreader's Marks

Change text:
You
~~It~~ should go.

Add text:
     she
She said ∧ will go.

See all Proofreader's Marks on page ix.

20 Use Subject Pronouns

Remember: The subject of a sentence can be a pronoun. A **subject pronoun** can be singular or plural.

- Use **I** when you talk about yourself.
- Use **you** to talk to one or more persons.
- Use **we** to talk about another person and yourself.
- Use **he, she, it,** and **they** to talk about other people or things.

  How do you know which pronoun to use? Look at the noun it goes with.

  1. If the noun is a man or boy, use **he**. If it is a woman or girl, use **she**.

  2. If the noun is a place or thing, use **it**. If the noun is plural, use **they**.

Try It

A. Complete each sentence. Write the correct subject pronoun.

1. Franco made a project for class. _____ He _____ worked on it for months.
    He / They

2. Sheila gave good advice. _____ She _____ said the project should be unique.
    He / She

3. Many students entered the science fair. _____ They _____ all worked hard.
    They / It

4. Franco's project was interactive. _____ He _____ thinks that added creativity.
    She / He

B. (5–9) Read the interview. Complete each sentence with the correct pronoun.

Q. How did you make your project the most creative at the science fair?

A. First, I chose an interesting subject. Then, my friend Sheila gave me advice.

_____ She _____ said my project should stand out. The other students and I discussed

creative ideas. _____ We _____ thought of many ways to make projects unique. I

decided to make my project an interactive experiment. The judges spent a long time at

my display. _____ They _____ said that my project was the most creative. The project took

weeks. _____ It _____ was worth it. The science fair was great. _____ It _____ was

more fun than I expected!

C. Answer the questions about a creative project you completed. Use subject pronouns.

10. What was the project you made? _____ made a _____.

11. Who gave you ideas about how to be creative? _____
    gave me creative ideas.

12. How did you feel about your project? _____ felt _____
    _____.

13. What did you learn from designing your project? _____
    _____

D. (14–16) Write at least three sentences that tell more about your creative
project. Use subject pronouns in your sentences.

_____

_____

_____

_____

Edit It

E. (17–20) Edit the article. Fix the four mistakes in pronouns.

Our sewing class put on a fashion show. It was very exciting.
First we sketched designs and made patterns. Then, we cut and
sewed our fabric. Everyone used their imaginations. ~~She~~ We wanted
the clothes to be original. Lydia won the Most Creative Design
award. ~~He~~ She designed the perfect outfit! She is in my group of
friends. ~~They~~ We are proud of her. Our principal Mr. Johannsen
was there. ~~They~~ He congratulated Lydia.

Proofreader's Marks

Change text:

She
~~It~~ ∧ won the award.

See all Proofreader's Marks
on page ix.

21 What Adds Action to a Sentence?

An Action Verb

- An **action verb** tells what the subject does.
  Some action verbs tell about an action that you cannot see.
  My parents **love** classical music.
  They **listen** to classical music on the radio all day.

- Make sure the action verb agrees with its subject. Add **-s** if the subject tells about one place, one thing, or one other person.
  I like many types of music.
  My **cousin listens** mostly to rap music.
  My **sister likes** country music best.
  We listen to several different radio stations.

Try It

A. Complete each sentence with an action verb. Possible responses:

1. Hip-hop songs _____tell_____ about the dreams and hardships of urban youth.

2. Classical pieces _____inspire_____ emotion through notes rather than words.

3. My neighbor _____listens_____ to jazz music.

4. I _____prefer_____ pop music.

5. My friends _____appreciate_____ songs with meaningful lyrics.

B. Complete each sentence with the correct form of the verb in parentheses.

6. My friends and I _____prefer_____ rock music to pop. **(prefer)**

7. My favorite singer _____sings_____ country songs. **(sing)**

8. Liliana _____memorizes_____ the lyrics of all her favorite songs. **(memorize)**

9. I _____like_____ the slower rhythm of country music. **(like)**

C. Answer the questions about music. Check that your verbs match their subjects.

10. What types of music do you and your friends listen to? My friends and I _____

_____.

11. Why do you like this type of music? _____ this music because

_____.

12. How do you feel when you hear your favorite songs? _____

_____

13. When do you listen to music? _____

_____

14. How does music affect other activities you do? _____

_____

15. How could you convince a family member to listen to your favorite type of music?

_____

_____

D. (16–20) Write at least five sentences about your family's favorite types of music. Use action verbs correctly in your sentences.

_____

_____

_____

_____

_____

_____

22 How Do You Know When the Action Happens?

Look at the Verb.

An **action verb** tells what the subject does. The tense of a verb tells when the action happens.

Present Tense

sing

sing**s**

Use the **present tense** to talk about actions that happen now or that happen on a regular basis.

My family **sings** in a choir together.

We **practice** at the community center once a week.

Try It

A. Complete each sentence with the correct form of the verb in parentheses.

1. My father _____drives_____ my family to choir practice. **(drive)**

2. We _____enjoy_____ singing together. **(enjoy)**

3. Sometimes my brother _____plays_____ the guitar while the choir sings. **(play)**

4. My brother and I _____like_____ to perform for large audiences. **(like)**

5. Our choir _____performs_____ several times each month. **(perform)**

B. (6–11) Complete each sentence with a verb from the box.

believes	feel	play	practice	takes	values

My family _____believes_____ that everyone should develop musical skills. My brother _____takes_____ guitar lessons. I _____practice_____ playing the drums. My sister and father _____play_____ the piano. We all _____feel_____ that music is an important part of life. Our family _____values_____ music.

C. Answer the questions about musical talents. Use present tense verbs in your answers.

12. What musical skills have you or your family learned through lessons and practice?

Through lessons and practice, _____.

13. How has learning about music benefited you? I have benefited because _____

_____.

14. In what other ways have you learned about music? _____

15. Would you recommend learning to play an instrument or taking singing lessons? _____

_____

16. Whose musical abilities do you admire? _____

17. How do you think developing musical talent affected this person? _____

_____

D. (18–20) Write at least three sentences about your experience learning about a certain style of music. Use present tense verbs correctly.

_____

_____

_____

E. (21–25) Edit the music review. Fix the five mistakes in present tense verb form.

Music Review

The family band called The Three of Us performs amazing shows. They shines on stage together. Ricardo play keyboard. His sister Marta sings and play guitar. Their uncle Daniel plays drums and sings, too. The family members writes and play their own music. They travel from city to city across the country. Audiences all over loves to see their shows.

Proofreader's Marks
Delete:
Greg and Suri raps well.
Add text:
He play the violin.
See all Proofreader's Marks on page ix.

48

23 Which Action Verbs End in -s?

The Ones That Go with He, She, or It

- An **action verb** in the **present tense** tells about something that happens now or on a regular basis.

- Add **-s** to the action verb if the subject tells about one place, one thing, or one other person.

  Tina listen**s** to music when she exercises. The music give**s** her energy.

  Sean keep**s** the radio on while driving. He turn**s** the volume low to be safe.

- If the verb ends in **sh, ch, ss, s, z,** or **x,** add **-es.**

  Sharese **relaxes** when she listens to songs with a slow rhythm.

  My family **teaches** me about music.

- Do not add **-s** to the action verb if the subject is **I, you, we, they,** or a plural noun.

  I **watch** my family. You could **learn** from them.

  The musicians **experiment** with different styles. They **get** feedback from the audience.

Try It

A. Complete each sentence about music. Write the correct form of the verb.

1. Music _____ affects _____ people's emotions and thoughts differently.
   affect / affects

2. It _____ helps _____ people in various ways.
   help / helps

3. People in my family _____ react _____ to music in different ways.
   react / reacts

4. My sister _____ watches _____ music videos to understand the messages of songs
   watch / watches
   more clearly.

5. When my brother wakes up to his favorite song, he energetically _____ springs _____
   spring / springs
   out of bed.

6. My aunt _____ misses _____ her high school friends when she hears certain songs.
   miss / misses

B. Complete each sentence with the correct form of the verb in parentheses.

7. I learn when I see how music ___influences___ other people. **(influence)**

8. My baby cousin ___falls___ asleep to soft music. **(fall)**

9. Now, when I have trouble going to sleep, I ___listen___ to music with a slow rhythm, too. **(listen)**

10. My brother ___stops___ listening to music when he does his homework. I tried turning off my MP3 player while working, and it helps me focus. **(stop)**

11. My sister ___watches___ her favorite music videos at the end of a hard day. She says they put her in a better mood. **(watch)**

Write It

C. Answer the questions about what you have learned about how people react to music. Use action verbs.

12. How do your friends react to upbeat music? My friends _____

_____.

13. What have you learned by watching friends about how people react to music? I learned

_____.

14. Describe how you react to music in different situations. _____

_____

15. In what situations does listening to music seem more or less helpful? _____

_____

D. (16–20) Write at least five more sentences about how people react to your favorite style of music. Use action verbs correctly in your sentences.

_____

_____

_____

_____

_____

24 What Kinds of Verbs Are Can, Could, May, and Might?

They Are Helping Verbs.

- An action verb can have two parts: a **helping verb** and a **main verb**. The main verb shows the action.

    I **play** drums. I **can** **play** drums.

- Some helping verbs change the meaning of the action verb.

    1. Use **can** or **could** to tell about an ability.

        Yesenia **can** **play** the guitar well. She **could** **teach** guitar lessons.

    2. Use **may**, **might**, or **could** to tell about a possibility.

        Raoul **may** learn to play the keyboards. He **might** **like** it. He **could** **begin** today.

- **Can**, **could**, **may**, and **might** stay the same with all subjects. Do not add **-s**.

    Oleg **plays** the saxophone. He **can** **help** other people learn. He **may** **suggest** that you learn.

Try It

A. Complete each sentence with can, could, may, or might. Possible responses:

1. Anna plays the guitar. She said she _____could_____ teach me, too.

2. I never considered playing the guitar, but Anna thinks I _____might_____ like it.

3. Anna _____can_____ teach me to play one song tomorrow after school.

4. If I don't like playing the guitar, I _____may_____ try to play a few different instruments.

B. (5–8) Read each sentence. Write whether it shows an ability or possibility. Then complete the sentences with the correct helping verb.

My friend Pavel plays drums. He (**might / can**) _____possibility; might_____ win a contest next week. Pavel said that anyone (**might / can**) _____ability; can_____ learn to play drums. He (**may / can**) _____possibility; may_____ teach me a few rhythms if we have time. Maybe I (**could / can**) _____possibility; could_____ learn to play drums, too.

C. Answer the questions about a person who has encouraged you to explore your musical interests. Use **can**, **could**, **may**, and **might** in your responses.

9. Who encouraged you to explore musical interests or abilities? _____ told me

_____.

10. What other musical abilities or interests might you explore? In the future, _____

_____.

11. Why might you explore those interests? _____

_____

12. What possibilities could learning music open for you? _____

_____

13. Can anyone develop musical talent? Why or why not? _____

_____

D. (14–16) Write at least three sentences about a creative talent you encouraged someone else to explore. Use **can**, **could**, **may**, and **might**.

_____

_____

_____

Edit It

E. (17–20) Edit the letter. Fix the four mistakes with helping verbs.

Dear Selma,

Thank you for giving me the idea to take voice lessons! I didn't think I could sing. I am surprised at the notes my voice may hit. Now I miht take more lessons. If so, I sing may in the school musical at the end of the year. Who knew that one suggestion coud make such a difference!

Sincerely,

Paula

Proofreader's Marks

Change text:
You might sing a wide range of notes.

Transpose words:
We play might in a band.

See all Proofreader's Marks on page ix.

52

25 Use Action Verbs in the Present Tense

Remember: A verb must agree with its subject.

- Some subjects take **-s** on the action verb.

I **play** songs.	He **plays** a song.
You **sing** along.	She **sings** along.
We **sound** great.	It **sounds** great.
They **clap** loudly.	A woman **claps** loudly.

- These verbs don't change. Do you know why?

  We **may play** for a group of senior citizens tomorrow.

  Our music **can help** them socialize and relax together.

  They **might ask** us to come again. It **could be** a regular gig.

Try It

A. Complete each sentence with the correct form of the verb.

1. My friend and I _____ write _____ songs together.
   write / writes

2. We _____ perform _____ the music at the elementary school.
   perform / performs

3. It _____ gives _____ the kids a time to relax and have fun.
   give / gives

4. They _____ smile _____ while we play.
   smile / smiles

5. Our music _____ makes _____ a difference to them.
   make / makes

B. Draw lines to logically connect the words in the first column with those in the second column.

6. My friend Suzy   might audition.

7. Her band   may record an album.

8. I'm a drummer, so I   sings for a band.

9. The band members   could sell quickly.

10. The band's CD   needs a new drummer.

Write It

C. Answer the questions about a way you or someone you know has used music to help others. Check that your verb forms match their subjects.

11. How did you or someone you know help others through music? Using music, _____

_____.

12. Why might music be helpful to this group of people? This _____ be helpful

because _____.

13. Why did you or this person want to help this group of people? _____

_____

14. Would you recommend that others get help through music? Why? _____

_____

D. (15–16) Write at least two sentences about another way you might help someone through music. Use present tense verbs correctly.

_____

_____

_____

Edit It

E. (17–20) Edit the article. Fix the four mistakes.

A local hip-hop band helps groups in the community. The
group visit the local senior citizen's center every Saturday.
                    s
The guys might dance as well as they sing, and they loves
           ^can
performing for audiences of all ages. If they can fit it into
                            may/might
their schedule, they can perform for the local high school
                        ^
during the homecoming game this fall.

Proofreader's Marks

Delete:

Most people likes music.

Add text:
       s
He help them through
        ^
music.

Change text:
     can
He may sing well.
    ^

See all Proofreader's Marks
on page ix.

54

26 What Forms of *Be* Are Used in the Present?

Am, *Is*, and *Are*

- Use the form of the verb **be** that matches the subject.

  I **am** talented at dancing.

  You **are** good at speaking in front of audiences.

  My friend Anna **is** an excellent gymnast.

  We **are** all skilled at different activities.

  My grandparents **are** both great at singing.

  You both **are** wonderful writers.

Present Tense Forms of *Be*
I **am**
he, she, or it **is**
we, you, or they **are**

- Use **not** after the verbs **am**, **is**, and **are** to make a sentence negative. The short form of **is not** is **isn't**. The short form of **are not** is **aren't**.

  1. He **is** not an actor.

     He **isn't** an actor.

  2. They **are** not musicians.

     They **aren't** musicians.

Try It

A. Write the correct form of the verb to complete the sentence.

1–2. My mother _____ is _____ an excellent writer. She _____ isn't _____
          is / are   isn't / isn't
very good at spelling, but she checks her work carefully.

3. I _____ am _____ good at telling jokes. My jokes make people laugh.
         am / are

4–5. You _____ are _____ a great speaker. Other students _____ aren't _____
          is / are   are / aren't
as calm as you are in front of large groups.

B. (6–11) Write the correct form of **be**.

My friends and I _____ are _____ talented at different things. I _____ am _____

a good dancer. Mark _____ isn't _____ as good at dancing, but he is excellent at drawing.

Belinda and Tyrone _____ are _____ great musicians. Belinda _____ is _____ an expert

piano player, and Tyrone _____ is _____ an amazing guitar player.

Write It

C. Answer the questions about creative skills and talents. Use correct forms of **be** in your answers.

12. Whose talent do you admire? I admire _____ because _____.

13. Describe what makes you creative. I _____ creative because _____.

14. What creative skill or talent would you like to develop? _____

15. How is being creative helpful to you? _____

D. (16–19) Write at least four sentences about a musician or musical group you admire. Use correct forms of the verb **be**.

_____

_____

_____

_____

Edit It

E. (20–25) Edit the journal entry. Fix the six mistakes with forms of the verb **be**.

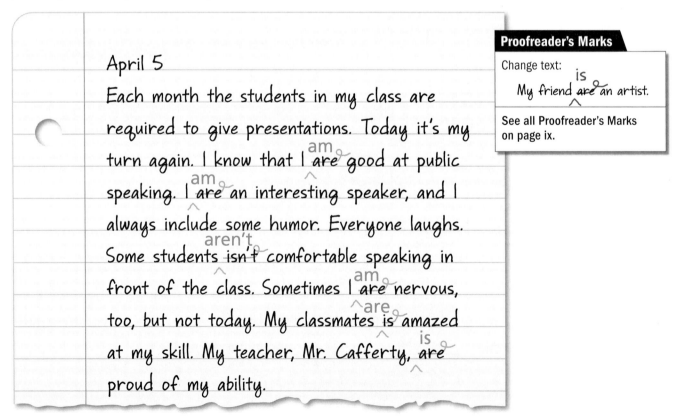

April 5

Each month the students in my class are required to give presentations. Today it's my turn again. I know that I ~~are~~ am good at public speaking. I ~~are~~ am an interesting speaker, and I always include some humor. Everyone laughs. Some students ~~isn't~~ aren't comfortable speaking in front of the class. Sometimes I ~~are~~ am nervous, too, but not today. My classmates ~~is~~ are amazed at my skill. My teacher, Mr. Cafferty, ~~are~~ is proud of my ability.

Proofreader's Marks

Change text:
                                is
My friend ~~are~~ an artist.

See all Proofreader's Marks on page ix.

56

27 How Do You Show That an Action Is in Process?

Use *Am*, *Is*, or *Are* plus the *-ing* Form of the Verb.

- The **present progressive** form of the verb ends in **-ing**.
- Use **am**, **is**, or **are** plus a **main verb** with **-ing** to show that an action is in the process of happening.
  The **helping verb** must agree with the subject.
  I **am** **writing** a new poem.
  The poem **is** **taking** a long time to write.
  My friends **are** **asking** to read it.
  They **are** **waiting** patiently to read the new poem.

Try It

A. Write the correct form of the present progressive to complete each sentence.

1. My friends and I ____are forming____ a band.
   is forming / are forming

2. I ____am playing____ percussion.
   am playing / are playing

3. Jorge and Delilah ____are singing____ the vocals.
   is singing / are singing

4. We ____are practicing____ after school today.
   is practicing / are practicing

5. The band ____is performing____ a variety of music.
   is performing / are performing

B. Draw lines to logically connect the words in the first column with those in the second column.

6. My classmates and I   am taking photographs of places in our city and school.

7. We   are forming a photography club.

8. I   is teaching us about our view of the world around us.

9. DeShaun   are planning to have an exhibit next month.

10. This project   is taking photos of his friends and family.

Write It

C. Answer the questions about a creative project that is teaching you about yourself or others. Use the present progressive in your responses.

11. What creative project are you working on now? I am _____

_____.

12. Who is helping you with the project? _____ me on my project.

13. What activities are others doing as part of the project? _____

_____

14. What are you learning about your own skills and talents? _____

_____

15. What is the project teaching you about working with others? _____

_____

D. (16–19) Write at least four sentences about any project you are currently involved in and what you are learning from it. Use the present progressive in your responses.

_____

_____

_____

_____

_____

Edit It

E. (20–25) Edit the radio commentary. Fix the six mistakes with the present progressive form.

Liam is describing the scene here at Fairview High for our radio listeners:

            is
"A young man ~~are~~ standing on a ladder in the cafeteria.
           ting
A female student is put∧tape around the windows. A group of
      ing   *ing* *are*
students are∧carry boxes. What are they do? They painting a
      are
mural! We ~~is~~ waiting anxiously to see it when it's done."

Proofreader's Marks
Add text: *ing* We are paint∧the gym.
Change text: *are* We ~~is~~ working hard.
See all Proofreader's Marks on page ix.

28 What Forms of *Have* Are Used in the Present?

Have and Has

Use the form of the verb **have** that matches the subject.

- I **have** a poem for the school literary magazine.
- He **has** an illustration.
- Our school **has** a literary arts club.
- We **have** talented students in our school.
- You **have** great writing talent, too.
- They **have** excellent drawing, writing, and advertising skills.

Present Tense Forms of *Have*
I **have**
he, she, or it **has**
we, you, or they **have**

Try It

A. Complete each sentence with have or has.

1. Our school _____has_____ a literary magazine.

2. The magazine _____has_____ a poetry section.

3. I _____have_____ a poem I might submit.

4. Do you _____have_____ a piece of writing that you would like to publish?

5. Lucinda _____has_____ a new story published in each issue.

B. Rewrite the sentences. Replace the underlined words with have or has.

6. My favorite song <u>contains</u> beautiful words. ____My favorite song has beautiful words.____

7. Song lyrics <u>possess</u> the same traits as poetry, such as rhyme and alliteration. ____Song lyrics have the same traits as poetry, such as rhyme and alliteration.____

8. I <u>wrote</u> a few poems that would make perfect song lyrics. ____I have a few poems that would make perfect song lyrics.____

C. Answer the questions about creative writing. Use **have** or **has** as needed.

9. What types of writing do you have experience with? I _____ experience writing

_____.

10. What creative writing journals or magazines does your school have? My school _____

_____

_____.

11. Why do you think your school has these publications? _____

_____

D. (12–15) Write at least four sentences about your own creative writing using **have** or **has**.

_____

_____

_____

_____

_____

Edit It

E. (16–20) Edit the introduction. Fix the five mistakes with **have** and **has**.

Introduction to This Issue

This edition of our literary magazine has two poems. Some
students think that poems always ~~have~~ words that rhyme at the
end of each line. Some poems ~~has~~ rhythm, but not rhyme. One
poem in this edition ~~have~~ words that rhyme. Another ~~has~~ a
conversational style without any rhythm or rhyme. The words
~~hav~~e meaning and a touching message. Read on, and enjoy the
words of your fellow students!

Proofreader's Marks

Add text:
                  has
This poem ∧ rhythm.

Change text:
                  has
My poem ~~have~~ rhyme.

See all Proofreader's Marks
on page ix.

29 What Forms of *Do* Are Used in the Present?

Do and Does

- Use the form of **do** that matches the subject. You can use **do** as a **main verb** or as a **helping verb**.

  I **do** my best at each audition.

  My mother **does** different things to help me.

  We **do hope** I can star in a musical one day.

  During rehearsal, we **do** every scene many times.

  The cast and crew **do** try their best to make the show a hit.

Present Tense Forms of *Do*
I **do**
he, she, or it **does**
we, you, or they **do**

- The short form of **does not** is **doesn't**. The short form of **do not** is **don't**.

  1. He **does not** sing well.

     He **doesn't** sing well.

  2. We **do not** want to miss the audition.

     We **don't** want to miss the audition.

Try It

A. Write the correct form of the verb to complete each sentence.

1. I _____ do _____ auditions for musicals about once a month.
   do / does

2. The directors _____ do _____ intimidate me sometimes.
   do / does

3. It _____ doesn't _____ stop me from trying.
   don't / doesn't

4. I _____ do _____ not have a song prepared for my audition tomorrow.
   do / does

5. My friend is also auditioning. We _____ do _____ hope that we both get a part.
   do / does

6. We still _____ don't _____ know where the theater is, but we will find out tonight.
   does not / don't

7. My mother will drive us to the theater. She _____ does _____ so much to help us audition.
   do / does

B. Choose words from each column to write five statements. You may use words more than once. Sentences will vary.

One thing I		every year is help with the school play.
Thierry and I always	does	the costumes and props.
But this year I	do	want to sew or build things.
This time, I will	don't	my best to get a small acting part.
Thierry		want to act in the play, too.

8. One thing I do every year is help with the school play.

9. Thierry and I always do the costumes and props.

10. But this year I don't want to sew or build things.

11. This time, I will do my best to get a small acting part.

12. Thierry does want to act in the play, too.

Write It

C. Answer the questions about performing. Use **do**, **don't**, **does**, or **doesn't** as needed in your responses.

13. What type of performing do you do? I _____.

14. How do you prepare for a performance? To prepare, I _____
_____

15. Why do people do auditions? _____

16. What do people do at auditions? _____

D. (17–20) Write at least four sentences about what you like or don't like about performing for an audience. Use forms of **do** and **do not** in your responses.

_____
_____
_____
_____
_____

30 Use Verbs to Talk About the Present

Remember: The verbs **be**, **have**, and **do** each have more than one form in the present. Use the form that goes with the subject.

Forms of *Be*	Forms of *Have*	Forms of *Do*
I **am**	I **have**	I **do**
he, she, or it **is**	he, she, or it **has**	he, she, or it **does**
we, you, or they **are**	we, you, or they **have**	we, you, or they **do**

Try It

A. Complete the sentences with the correct present tense form of the verb in parentheses.

1. Our classmates _____ are _____ enthusiastic about literary arts. **(be)**

2. I _____ am _____ the editor of our school magazine. **(be)**

3. Diego _____ does _____ the proofreading for the magazine. **(do)**

4. I _____ have _____ respect for anyone who writes poems. **(have)**

5. This year the school _____ has _____ a group of students who are putting together a poetry slam. **(have)**

6. They _____ are _____ poets who have participated in poetry slams. **(be)**

7. During the poetry slam, each poet _____ has _____ a turn on stage. **(have)**

8. The students _____ do _____ the decorations for the event. **(do)**

9. We _____ are _____ so excited about hearing our schoolmates do poetry slams on stage! **(be)**

10. We _____ do _____ hope the slam is a success **(do)**

B. (11–16) Read the interview. Write the correct verb to complete the sentence.

Q. Why do you do poetry slams?

A. I _____ have _____ a lot of encouragement for my poetry. My brother and I
　　　　　 have / has
enter poetry slams together on the weekends. My brother _____ has _____
　　　　　　　　　　　　　　　　　　　　　　　　　　　　　 have / has
a part-time job, so I _____ do _____ more preparing for the contests than
　　　　　　　　　　 do / does
he does. He _____ has _____ a lot of fun doing slams anyway.
　　　　　 have / has
They _____ are _____ a good way to develop our talent with poetry
　　　 are / am
and rhythm. We _____ are _____ more confident because of this hobby.
　　　　　　　 is / are

Write It

C. Answer the questions about your experience with poetry or events like poetry slams. Use forms of **be**, **have**, and **do**.

17. Are poetry slams more popular than poetry readings? _____

_____

18. When have you read, written, or spoken poetry? _____

_____

19. What are your feelings and thoughts about poetry? _____

_____

20. Who is your favorite poet? What is your favorite poem? _____

_____

D. (21–25) Write at least five more sentences that describe your experience with poetry. Use the correct forms of **be**, **have**, and **do**.

_____

_____

_____

_____

_____

_____

✓ Capitalize the Names of Groups

- The names of some groups are proper nouns and should be capitalized. A **proper noun** is a noun that names a specific person, place, or thing. These include institutions, businesses, organizations, and government agencies.
  Institution: Newberry Public Library
  Business: Fig Media Incorporated
  Organization: National High School Association
- The names of nonspecific groups should not be capitalized.
  a library
  a company
  an association

Try It

A. Use proofreader's marks to correct the capitalization error in each sentence.

Proofreader's Marks
Capitalize:
I work at edge hair salon.
Do not capitalize:
I work at a Hair Salon.
See all Proofreader's Marks on page ix.

1. Our school uniforms are made at American Uniform association. It is one of the largest uniform Companies in the country.

2. Our school is the only school in district 12 that requires school uniforms. The other districts do not have a school uniform policy.

B. (3–10) Edit the letter. Fix the eight mistakes in capitalization.

Dear Ms. Gomez:

   As a Member of the Student Council, I do not think our school should require students to wear uniforms. Other Districts do not require students to wear uniforms. In fact, district 16 has issued school dress codes to solve the clothing problem. We propose that a dress code, not a uniform policy, be issued for Glendale High school.

Sincerely,

Yvonne Gustin

Vice President, Glendale high school Student Council

✔Use Colons Correctly

- Use a **colon** after a complete sentence to set off a list of items, an explanation, or a quotation.

  You must wear the new school uniform: long pants or a skirt below the knee, a shirt with a collar, and a pair of loafers.

  The new rule is simple: You must wear the uniform whenever you are at school.

- Capitalize the first word after a colon if it is a **proper noun** or the first word of a complete sentence.

  Three students helped write the dress code rules: **Anika**, Tom, and Sam.

  They added the following rule: **Students** must also follow the dress code during school-sponsored outings.

Try It

A. For each sentence, add a colon or capitalize a word.

11. Our high school has a new dress code: students cannot wear clothing that is inappropriate or offensive.

12. Students are not allowed to wear baseball caps, tank tops, shorts, or T-shirts with words or pictures.

13. Our school handbook lists one exception: "On half days, students may wear jeans and non-offensive T-shirts."

Proofreader's Marks
Add a colon:
These students have already bought their uniforms: Valerie, Sam, and Angel.
Capitalize:
There's a new rule: you can't wear flip-flops.

B. Write two sentences that contain a list of reasons why you do or do not want to wear a school uniform. One sentence should have a colon; the other should not. Sentences will vary.

14. _____

_____

15. _____

_____

✓ Check Your Spelling

Homonyms are words that sound alike but have different meanings and spellings. Spell these homonyms correctly when you proofread.

Homonyms and Their Meanings	Examples
to (preposition) = toward	Tiana went **to** a new school.
two (adjective) = the number 2	The book has **two** parts.
too (adverb) = also, more than enough	The rule is **too** strict.
your (adjective) = belonging to you	**Your** report was interesting.
you're (contraction) = you are	**You're** the first person in line.

Try It

A. Complete each sentence about school uniforms. Use the correct homonym.

16. Unfortunately, the company charges _____ too _____ much
        for the uniforms.
        to / two / too

17. How can you afford _____ your _____ uniform at those prices?
        your / you're

18. You have to buy your own socks, _____ too _____.
        to / two / too

19. The worst thing about wearing a school uniform is that you lose
        _____ your _____ freedom of expression.
        your / you're

20. Clothes and jewelry allow us _____ to _____ be creative.
        to / two / too

B. (21–23) Do you think schools should issue a uniform policy, create a dress
code, or allow students to wear whatever they want to wear? Write at least
three sentences. Be sure to use one homonym in each sentence. Sentences will vary.

_____

_____

_____

_____

✓ Use Correct Verb Forms in the Present Tense

- **Have**, **be**, and **do** are irregular verbs. They have more different forms in their present tense than regular verbs do.

    I **have** a dress code at school. She has one, too.

    Are you satisfied with the decision? **Is** your friend satisfied? I definitely **am**.

    I **do** own a uniform. So **does** he.

- Use **not** after each form of **be** or **do** to make a sentence negative.

    She **is not** happy. She **does not** want to wear a uniform.

Forms of *Have*
I, we, you, or they **have**
he, she, or it **has**

Forms of *Be*
I **am**
he, she, or it **is**
we, you, or they **are**

Forms of *Do*
I, we, you, or they **do**
he, she, or it **does**

Try It

A. (24–28) Edit the paragraph. Fix the five verbs that do not match their subjects.

<u>High School Dress Code Policy:</u> Students ~~is~~ **are** to follow the dress code at all times. If they ~~doesn't~~ **don't** wear the proper attire, then they aren't following the dress code. No student ~~have~~ **has** permission to disobey the code. There ~~is~~ **are** no exceptions to the rule. The dress code ~~are~~ **is** a necessary part of a positive learning environment for students.

Proofreader's Marks

Delete:
I like your new ~~new~~ uniform.

Add text:
                did
Where ∧ you buy your uniform?

B. (29–30) Write at least two sentences telling how students, teachers, and parents might feel about the dress code policy. Use a form of the verb **have**, **be**, or **do** in each sentence.   Sentences will vary.

_____

_____

_____

31 How Do You Show That an Action Already Happened?

Add -ed to the Verb.

The **tense** of a verb shows when an action happens.

- Action in the **present tense** happens now or on a regular basis.
- Action in the **past tense** happened earlier.

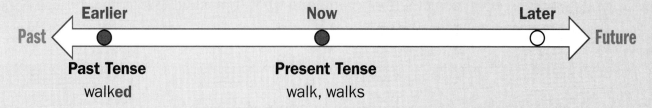

Earlier	**Now**	**Later**

Past ⟵ ━━━━━━━━━━━━━━━━━━━━━━━━━━━━ ⟶ Future

Past Tense
walk**ed**

Present Tense
walk, walks

Add -**ed** to most verbs when you talk about a past action.

1. Today, Tomás **walks** home from work.
   Yesterday, Tomás **walked** home, too.

2. Today, he **smells** smoke.
   Yesterday, he **smelled** smoke, too.

Try It

A. Complete each sentence with the past tense of the verb in parentheses.

1. Tomás _____passed_____ the corner and saw a house on fire. **(pass)**

2. A woman _____screamed_____ that her child was inside. **(scream)**

3. Tomás _____entered_____ the house. **(enter)**

4. "Help me!" _____yelled_____ a voice. **(yell)**

B. (5–8) Complete each sentence with a past tense. Possible responses:

Tomás _____looked_____ for the child. He _____turned_____ to see a little boy.
Tomás _____picked_____ up the boy. He _____rushed_____ outside with the child.

C. Answer the questions about Tomás's story. Use the past tense.

9. What did Tomás do that was brave? He _____

_____.

10. What was it like inside the burning house? Smoke _____

_____.

11. Would you have done something different than what Tomás did? Write about it using the
past tense. _____

_____

D. **(12–14)** Think about a time when you or someone you know was brave.
Write at least three sentences telling what happened. Use the past tense.

_____

_____

_____

_____

_____

Edit It

E. **(15–20)** Edit the journal entry. Fix six mistakes with verbs.

August 10

Yesterday, it rained all day. The streets filled
with water, and soon the river flooded. When
                          reached   climbed
the water reaches the front door, we climb
                    watched
onto the roof. We watch as many things
floated   helped
float by. Some men in a boat help us escape.
      thanked
We thank them many times.

Proofreader's Marks

Change text:
             sighed
They sigh when it was
over. ∧

See all Proofreader's Marks
on page ix.

32 Can You Just Add -ed to Form a Verb in the Past?

Not Always

Most verbs end with **-ed** to show the past tense. Sometimes you have to change the spelling of the verb before you add **-ed**.

1. If a verb ends in silent **e**, drop the **e**. Then add **-ed**.

   My grandmother liv**ed** in a small village when she was younger. **(live)**

   The people in the village relat**ed** this story for many years. **(relate)**

2. Some one-syllable verbs end in one vowel and one consonant. Double the consonant before you add **-ed**.

   There were men who robb**ed** villages. **(rob)**

   The story tells how a girl stopp**ed** these robbers. **(stop)**

Try It

A. Complete each sentence with the past tense of the verb in parentheses.

1. One day, at home alone, the girl ____noticed____ some strangers coming. **(notice)**

2. She ____believed____ they were robbers. **(believe)**

3. The girl ____planned____ how to stop them. **(plan)**

4. She ____grabbed____ a white cloth. **(grab)**

5. Then she ____raced____ outside. **(race)**

6. The robbers saw the house was empty and ____stayed____. **(stay)**

B. (7–11) Complete each sentence with a past tense verb. Possible responses:

At dusk, the girl ____slipped____ behind the house. She ____tapped____ on the walls and moans. She ____waved____ the white cloth like it was a ghost. She ____scared____ the robbers so much that they left the village. The villagers ____named____ the girl Clever One.

C. Answer the questions. Use the past tense.

12. What do you think the robbers did when they thought they saw a ghost? They _____
_____ .

13. What do you think the girl did after the robbers left? She _____
_____ .

D. (14–17) Think about a story you have heard about a hero or legend. Write at least four sentences telling the main events in the story. Use the past tense.

_____

_____

_____

_____

_____

Edit It

E. (18–25) Edit the journal entry. Fix eight mistakes with verbs.

January 14

Last week, it snowed so much that no one
dared
~~dares~~ go out. We ~~use~~ used up all our food, so
decided
Father ~~decides~~ to go to town. Ice ~~covers~~ covered the
slipped
roads. The horse ~~slips~~ on the ice, so Father
walked
~~walks~~ many miles to the store. Then he ~~drags~~ dragged
a box of food back to us through the snow.
opened
Finally, he ~~open~~ the door.

Proofreader's Marks
Change text:
closed We ~~close~~ the door after Father.
See all Proofreader's Marks on page ix.

33 When Do You Use *Was* and *Were*?

When You Tell About the Past

The verb **be** has special forms to tell about the present and the past.

	Earlier	Now	Later	
Past ←	●	●	○	→ Future

Past Tense
I **was**
you **were**
he, she, or it **was**
we **were**
they **were**

Present Tense
I **am**
you **are**
he, she, or it **is**
we **are**
they **are**

Present: Our school's soccer team **is** not very good.

Past: Last year, it **was** the worst team in the league.

Present: Our athletes **are** always surprised when they do well.

Past: They **were** really surprised when Felipe scored the winning goal.

Try It

A. Rewrite each sentence using the past tense of the <u>verb</u>.

1. It <u>is</u> our first game of the season. <u>It was our first game of the season.</u>

2. We <u>are</u> behind. <u>We were behind.</u>

3. There <u>are</u> only two minutes left. <u>There were only two minutes left.</u>

4. Felipe <u>is</u> in the middle of the field when he got the ball. <u>Felipe was in the middle of the field when he got the ball.</u>

5. His teammates <u>are</u> excited and yelled for him to pass it. <u>His teammates were excited and yelled for him to pass it.</u>

B. (6–13) Complete each sentence with the correct form of the past tense of **be**.

Felipe _____was_____ small but quick. Two guys from the other team _____were_____ in his way. Felipe kicked the ball and leaped between them. It looked like he _____was_____ in the air! When he landed, he _____was_____ able to kick the ball into the goal. All the fans _____were_____ excited because the teams had tied. At the kick-off, Felipe _____was_____ the first to get the ball. We _____were_____ amazed to see him dribble it and score again. It _____was_____ unbelievable!

Write It

C. Answer the questions. Use **was** and **were** in your answers.

14. Write about your response to Felipe's part in the soccer game. _____

_____

15. How might people exaggerate what Felipe did in the game? _____

_____

16. Why might people want to exaggerate? _____

_____

D. (17–20) Think about someone you know who did something amazing. Write at least four sentences telling what happened. Use **was** and **were**.

_____

_____

_____

_____

_____

34 When Do You Use *Had*?

When You Tell About the Past

The verb **have** uses special forms to show the present and the past.

Earlier	**Now**	**Later**

Past ⟵ ● ——————— ● ——————————— ○ ⟶ Future

Past Tense	**Present Tense**
I **had**	I **have**
you **had**	you **have**
he, she, or it **had**	he, she, or it **has**
we **had**	we **have**
they **had**	they **have**

Present: We **have** a new teacher.

Past: We **had** a new teacher.

Present: She **has** a book about World War II.

Past: She **had** a book about World War II.

Try It

A. Rewrite each sentence, changing the <u>verb</u> to the past tense.

1. The book <u>has</u> many interesting stories. _The book had many interesting stories._

2. It <u>has</u> photos of real heroes. _It had photos of real heroes._

3. They <u>have</u> frightening experiences. _They had frightening experiences._

4. One family <u>has</u> a difficult decision to make. _One family had a difficult decision to make._

5. They <u>have</u> friends who were in great danger. _They had friends who were in great danger._

B. (6–14) Complete each sentence with the past tense of **have**.

The family _____had_____ a place for their friends to hide. Their friends _____had_____ nowhere else to go. The family _____had_____ to keep the hiding place a secret or they would be in danger, too. The family _____had_____ to bring food and water to their hidden friends. The friends _____had_____ to be silent so no one would find them. But they _____had_____ a little boy. One day, he _____had_____ a fever. The family _____had_____ to find a doctor who could be trusted. Luckily, the people in hiding survived. When the war ended, they _____had_____ a celebration to thank the family for saving their lives.

Write It

C. Answer the questions. Use the past tense of **have** in your answers.

15. Why were the people in the family heroes? The family _____

_____.

16. What do you think the people in hiding said about the family after the war? They _____

_____.

D. (17–20) Think about a person or group that acted heroically in the past. Write at least four sentences telling what they did. Use the past tense of **have** in your answers.

_____

_____

_____

_____

_____

_____

35 Use Verb Tenses

Remember: You have to change the verb to show the past tense.

Add **-ed** to most verbs. You may need to make a spelling change before you add **-ed**.

Present Tense	Past Tense
work, works	worked
want, wants	wanted
drag, drags	dragged
live, lives	lived

Use special forms for the past tense of **be** and **have**.

Forms of *Be*

Present Tense	Past Tense
am, is, are	was, were

Forms of *Have*

Present Tense	Past Tense
have, has	had

Try It

A. Complete each sentence with the correct form of the verb.

1. Last year, I _____ had _____ an assignment to write about a hero.
   have / had

2. I _____ decided _____ to research Cesar Chavez.
   decide / decided

3. I _____ learned _____ that Cesar Chavez and his family _____ were _____
   learn / learned   are / were
   migrant farm workers.

4. Cesar Chavez _____ started _____ a union for farm workers in 1962.
   start / started

B. Complete each sentence with the past tense of the verb in parentheses.

5. Chavez _____ wanted _____ better conditions for farm workers. **(want)**

6. Many farm workers _____ joined _____ the union. **(join)**

7. Some grape growers _____ refused _____ to listen to the union. **(refuse)**

8. Chavez _____ asked _____ people to boycott the grape growers. **(ask)**

C. Answer the questions. Use the past tense.

9. Cesar Chavez believed in nonviolence, even when others behaved violently. How do you think this helped the farm workers? I think _____

_____.

10. Do you think it was hard to be nonviolent? _____

_____

11. What do you think would have happened if the union members had acted violently?

_____

_____

D. **(12–14) What do you think about Cesar Chavez? Write at least three sentences explaining your opinion. Use the past tense in some of your sentences.**

_____

_____

_____

_____

_____

_____

Edit It

E. **(15–20) Edit the paragraph. Fix six mistakes with verbs.**

When Cesar Chavez was a boy, his family moved around
California. They have to go where there is work for them.
          had   was
Cesar pick fruits and vegetables in many places. He work
      picked   worked
very long days. He helped his family and earn money. This was
                                          earned
the beginning of a life spent helping others. He want to help
                                                 wanted
migrant farm workers.

Proofreader's Marks
Change text: *worked*
Cesar Chavez work hard.
See all Proofreader's Marks on page ix.

78

36 How Do You Show That an Action Already Happened?

Change the Verb.

Add **-ed** to most verbs to show that an action already happened.
Use special past tense forms for **irregular verbs.**

Present	Past	Example in the Past
ring	rang	The fire alarm **rang** in the middle of the night.
bring	brought	The alarm **brought** my dad to his feet.
know	knew	Dad and the other firefighters **knew** what to do.
get	got	They **got** dressed.
find	found	They **found** their gear.
go, goes	went	Then they **went** to the fire truck.
stand	stood	Dad **stood** in the back of the truck.
see	saw	Then they **saw** the house on fire.

Try It

A. Rewrite each sentence changing the <u>verb</u> to the past tense.

1. The firefighters <u>know</u> what to do. _The firefighters knew what to do._

2. They <u>have</u> little time to do it. _They had little time to do it._

3. They <u>get</u> out the hoses. _They got out the hoses._

4. Some of the firefighters <u>stand</u> with the hoses outside the house. _Some of the firefighters stood with the hoses outside the house._

5. Then they <u>see</u> a man who said there was someone inside. _Then they saw a man who said there was someone inside._

79

B. Complete each sentence with the past tense of the verb in parentheses.

6. Dad _____got_____ a mask to help with breathing. **(get)**

7. Then he _____went_____ into the building. **(go)**

8. He _____knew_____ he had to hurry. **(know)**

9. He _____found_____ a man inside. **(find)**

10. Dad _____brought_____ the man out. **(bring)**

Write It

C. Answer the questions. Use some irregular verbs in the past tense.

11. How did Dad find the man in the building? He _____

_____.

12. What did the firefighters do that was heroic? They _____

_____.

D. (13–16) Think about someone in your community whose job required him or her to be brave. Write at least four sentences telling what this person did that was heroic. Use the past tense of some irregular verbs.

_____

_____

_____

_____

_____

Edit It

E. (17–20) Edit the news report. Fix four mistakes.

Yesterday, there was an accident. A truck ~~goes~~ went off the road. They ~~find~~ found the driver asleep at the wheel. Paramedics ~~come~~ came and treated the driver. Then they ~~bringed~~ brought him to the hospital.

Proofreader's Marks

Change text:

They ~~come~~ came in time to help.

See all Proofreader's Marks on page ix.

80

㊲ How Do You Show That an Action Already Happened?

Change the Verb.

Add **-ed** to most verbs to show that an action already happened.
Use special past tense forms for **irregular verbs**.

Present	Past	Example in the Past
take	took	My grandmother **took** me under her wing.
read	read	She **read** me stories about people who were kind.
say	said	She **said** kind people could be heroes.
tell	told	She **told** me that I could be a hero, too.
make	made	Her words **made** a big impression on me.
feel	felt	I **felt** like helping others.
speak	spoke	I was glad she **spoke** to me like that.
keep	kept	I always **kept** her words in mind.

Try It

A. Complete each sentence with the past tense of the verb in parentheses.

1. My grandmother _____gave_____ me some money for my birthday. **(give)**

2. I _____kept_____ the money for a while. **(keep)**

3. Then I _____knew_____ what to buy. **(know)**

4. On my way to the store, I _____saw_____ a homeless man. **(see)**

5. He _____stood_____ with a sign asking for food. **(stand)**

B. Rewrite each sentence, changing the <u>verb</u> to the past tense.

6. I <u>hide</u> my money at first. <u>I hid my money at first.</u>

7. Then, I <u>feel</u> bad. <u>Then, I felt bad.</u>

8. I <u>take</u> some sandwiches to the man. <u>I took some sandwiches to the man.</u>

9. He <u>tells</u> me he had not eaten for two days. <u>He told me he had not eaten for two days.</u>

10. He <u>says</u> I saved his life. <u>He said I saved his life.</u>

Write It

C. Answer the questions. Use the past tense of some irregular verbs.

11. Do you think the narrator acted heroically? Why or why not? I think _____.

12. What do you think the homeless man did after the narrator gave him food? He _____.

D. (13–15) Think about a time that you did a small act that made a big difference. Write at least three sentences telling what happened. Use the past tense of some irregular verbs.

_____

_____

_____

_____

_____

38 How Do You Show That an Action Was In Process?

Use *Was* or *Were* Plus the *-ing* Form of the Verb.

- Sometimes you want to show that an action was happening over a period of time in the past. Use the past progressive form of the verb.

- To form the past progressive, use the helping verb **was** or **were** plus a main verb that ends in **-ing**. The helping verb must agree with the subject.

  Shawna **was planning** to enter the dance competition.
  I **was helping** her with her moves.
  Some other girls **were teasing** Shawna.
  They **were saying** she was not a good dancer.
  Everyone **was thinking** these girls would win.

Try It

A. Complete each sentence with the past progressive form of the verb in parentheses.

1. Shawna _____was feeling_____ badly. **(feel)**

2. She _____was thinking_____ that the girls were right. **(think)**

3. "I _____was forgetting_____ my steps," she said. **(forget)**

4. "Those girls _____were watching_____ me." **(watch)**

5. "I know they _____were laughing_____ at me." **(laugh)**

6. I said, "They _____were trying_____ to lower your confidence." **(try)**

7. "They _____were hoping_____ that you would drop out." **(hope)**

8. I _____was telling_____ Shawna that she was a good dancer. **(tell)**

9. Finally, Shawna _____was listening_____ to me. **(listen)**

10. At the competition, she _____was smiling_____ when she went onstage. **(smile)**

B. Rewrite each sentence using the past progressive of the <u>verb</u>.

11. My brother <u>worries</u> about his math test. _My brother was worrying about his_ _math test._

12. He <u>studies</u> all night. _He was studying all night._

13. His friends <u>make</u> fun of him. _His friends were making fun of him._

14. I <u>encourage</u> him not to give up. _I was encouraging him not to give up._

15. I <u>help</u> him study the night before the test. _I was helping him study the night_ _before the test._

Write It

C. Answer the questions. Use the past progressive tense of verbs in your answers.

16. What do you think happened to Shawna during the dance competition? Shawna _____

_____ .

17. How have you encouraged a friend to do something? I _____

_____ .

D. **(18–20) Think about a time when someone encouraged you. Write at least three sentences telling what happened. Use the past progressive tense in some of your sentences.**

_____

_____

_____

_____

_____

39 How Do You Tell About the Future?

Use *Will* Before the Verb.

The **future tense** of a verb shows that an action will happen later.

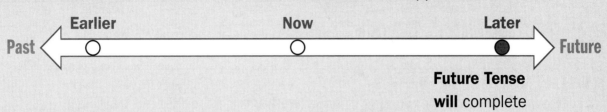

- To form the future tense, use **will** before the main verb.
  We **will complete** safety training at work.
- You can also use **am, is**, or **are** plus **going to** before the main verb.
  We **are going to complete** safety training at work.

Try It

A. Complete each sentence. Use the future tense of the verb in parentheses.
More than one answer is possible. Possible responses:

1. We _____will learn_____ how to stay safe in a restaurant kitchen. **(learn)**

2. The manager ___is going to show___ a video about handling food safely. **(show)**

3. The head cook ___will demonstrate___ how to put out a grease fire. **(demonstrate)**

4. We _____will use_____ the fire extinguisher. **(use)**

5. We _____will take_____ a test to show what we learned. **(take)**

B. Complete each sentence. Use the future tense of a verb from the box. More than
one answer is possible. Possible responses:

be	help	know	tell

6. Learning about safety ___will help___ us in an emergency.

7. We ___will know___ what to do if someone gets hurt.

8. We ___will be___ more careful in the kitchen now.

C. Answer the questions. Use future tense verbs in your sentences.

9. How will taking a CPR class help a babysitter? It _____

_____.

10. How will first-aid training help people who work at the mall? They _____

_____.

11. How could someone working in an office benefit from first-aid training? _____

_____.

D. (12–16) What are your plans for learning how to act in an emergency?
Write at least five sentences telling what you will do to prepare yourself for
emergencies. Use future tense verbs in your sentences.

_____

_____

_____

_____

_____

_____

Edit It

E. (17–20) Edit the class description. Use the future tense with will. Fix four
mistakes.

Basic Life Guarding 101

This class will teach water safety to people who wish to lifeguard.
~~will learn~~
Students ~~learn~~ the basics of water rescue. They ~~demonstrate~~ *will demonstrate*

their knowledge of water safety. Instructors ~~present~~ material *will present*
will have to
in various ways. Students ~~have to~~ pass a test at the end of the

class.

Proofreader's Marks

Change text:
will help
It ~~help~~ me at work.

See all Proofreader's Marks
on page ix.

40 Use Verb Tenses

Remember: You have to change the verb to show when an action happens. The action can happen in the **present**, **past**, or **future**.

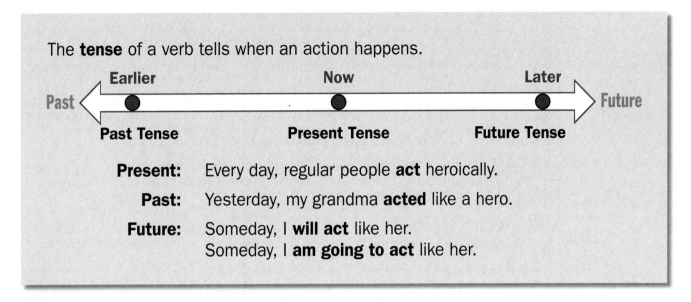

The **tense** of a verb tells when an action happens.

Earlier — Now — Later

Past ← Past Tense — Present Tense — Future Tense → Future

Present: Every day, regular people **act** heroically.

Past: Yesterday, my grandma **acted** like a hero.

Future: Someday, I **will act** like her.
Someday, I **am going to act** like her.

Try It

A. Complete each sentence. Use the correct tense of the verb in parentheses.

1. Yesterday, my grandmother ___was driving___ home. **(past progressive of drive)**

2. She ___saw___ a car crash into a pole. **(past tense of see)**

3. The driver ___was calling___ for help. **(past progressive of call)**

4. "I ___will help___ you," Grandma said. **(future tense of help)**

B. Complete each sentence with the correct tense of a verb from the box. More than one answer is possible. Possible responses:

help	know	limp	save

5. Grandma ___knew___ she had to act quickly.

6. She ___helped___ the driver out of the car.

7. He ___was limping___, but he was smiling, too.

8. "You ___saved___ my life," he told Grandma.

C. Answer the questions. Use different tenses to make your meaning clear.

9. Why did the narrator want to be like his or her grandma? The narrator _____

_____.

10. What do you think will happen to the injured driver? I think _____

_____.

D. (11–13) Think about an ordinary person you know who is a hero. Write at least three sentences telling what this person has done in the past and what you think he or she will do in the future. Use different tenses to make your meaning clear.

_____

_____

_____

_____

_____

Edit It

E. (14–20) Edit the story. Fix seven mistakes in verb tense. More than one answer is possible in the last sentence. Possible responses:

Rollo the Wonder Dog

Yesterday was an extraordinary day. Rollo ~~know~~ knew something was wrong. Grandpa ~~lies~~ was lying on the floor. Rollo ~~bark~~ barked all morning. Finally, a neighbor ~~come~~ came to see what was wrong. Grandpa ~~breathe~~ was breathing, but he was very ill.

"You ~~live~~ will live," the neighbor ~~tell~~ told him, "thanks to Rollo the Wonder Dog!"

Proofreader's Marks

Change text:
The neighbor ~~hear~~ heard Rollo barking.

See all Proofreader's Marks on page ix.

41 How Do Nouns Work in a Sentence?

They Can Be the Subject or the Object.

- Nouns can be the **subject** of a sentence.

    Teens have a bad reputation.
    subject

- Nouns can also be the **object** of an action verb. To find the object, turn the verb into a question like: "Distrust whom?"
    Your answer is the object.

    Many adults distrust **teens**.
    verb   object

- Many English sentences follow this pattern: **subject → verb → object**.

    Some teens cause problems.
    subject   verb   object

    But my friends helped our community.
    subject   verb   object

Try It

A. Read each sentence. Write whether the underlined noun is a subject or an object.

1. Many <u>parents</u> have jobs. _____subject_____

2. Their children take the <u>bus</u> home after school. _____object_____

3. No one is able to watch these <u>kids</u>. _____object_____

4. Some <u>kids</u> need help with homework. _____subject_____

5. Other children make <u>trouble</u>. _____object_____

6. My <u>friends</u> started a club for kids after school. _____subject_____

7. A neighbor offered a <u>room</u>. _____object_____

8. The grocer donated <u>snacks</u>. _____object_____

9. The teens give <u>help</u> to the kids. _____object_____

10. These <u>teens</u> solved a social problem. _____subject_____

Write It

B. Choose an object from the box to complete each sentence.

article	cans	example	garden
meals	principal	program	students

11. Our school has a _____program_____ to fight hunger.

12. Some students prepare _____meals_____ for elderly people who can't cook.

13. One class distributes _____cans_____ of food.

14. The science class planted a _____garden_____ for the community.

15. A reporter wrote an _____article_____ about our program.

16. Other schools followed our _____example_____.

17. The mayor thanked the _____students_____ for their work.

18. She congratulated our _____principal_____, too.

C. Answer the questions. Be sure your sentences contain a subject and an object.

19. What have you done to work for social change? I _____

_____.

20. What could the people in your community do to create social change? _____

_____

D. (21–25) What laws or situations would you like to change in your community?
Write at least five sentences telling what you would change and why. Use
subjects and objects in your sentences.

_____

_____

_____

_____

_____

_____

42 Why Are There So Many Pronouns?

Some Work as Subjects, and Some Work as Objects.

- Use a **subject pronoun** as the subject of a sentence.

  My uncle **Steve** believes in equality. **He** fought for civil rights.
  <small>subject</small>

  The **civil rights movement** happened in the 1960s. **It** was an important time.
  <small>subject</small>

- Use an **object pronoun** as the object of the verb.

  Many people disliked segregation. These people fought against **it**.
  <small>object</small>

Pronouns	
Subject	**Object**
I	me
you	you
he	him
she	her
it	it

  Steve helped to register voters. Some people distrusted **him**.
  <small>object</small>

- The pronouns **you** and **it** stay the same as subjects and objects.

Try It

A. Complete each pair of sentences with a pronoun. Circle the noun from the first sentence that the pronoun refers to.

1. One man shouted at (Steve). The man called _____him_____ names.

2. Some kids tried to beat up (Steve). Luckily, _____he_____ wasn't hurt.

3. Steve talked to an elderly (woman). _____She_____ had never voted before.

4. Steve handed (Mrs. Hill) a form. Steve told _____her_____ the form would let her vote.

B. (5–9) Complete the sentences with subject and object pronouns.

A newspaper published a letter to the editor. _____It_____ said that some people shouldn't be allowed to vote. Steve read the article. _____It_____ made _____him_____ mad. _____He_____ called the woman who wrote the letter. Steve told _____her_____ that everyone had the right to vote.

C. Answer the questions. Use subject and object pronouns.

10. How did Steve make changes in our country? He _____

_____.

11. Why is voting important? It _____

_____.

12. What would you like to say to Steve? You _____

_____.

D. (13–15) Think about someone whose actions helped change history. Write at least three sentences telling what happened. Use subject and object pronouns.

_____

_____

_____

_____

_____

_____

Edit It

E. (16–20) Edit the letter. Fix five mistakes with pronouns.

Dear Steve,

    My mother asked me to thank you. Steve helped she vote.
(You, me)   (she)   (her)
Mother told I that the first time her voted was special. He was
               (It)
the most important day in her life. She will never forget it.

Voting is an important responsibility. Everyone who is eligible

should vote!

Sincerely,

Sally Hill

Proofreader's Marks

Change text:
She
~~Her~~ wanted to thank
you.

See all Proofreader's Marks on page ix.

92

43 Do You Ever Talk About Yourself?

Then Learn to Use the Words *I* and *Me*.

Subject Pronoun: I

- Use the pronoun **I** in the **subject** of a sentence.

    I like Angelo's Grocery.

- In a compound subject, name yourself last.

    Correct: **Tess and I** go there after school.

    She and I like to buy a snack.

    Incorrect: Me and Tess like Mr. Angelo.

Object Pronoun: me

- Use the pronoun **me** as the **object**. Mr. and Mrs. Angelo are friendly to **me**.

- In a compound object, name yourself last.

    Correct: Mrs. Angelo smiles at **Tess and me**.

    Mr. Angelo says hello to **her and me**.

    Incorrect: Mr. Angelo gave samples to Tess and I.

    He asked me and her if they were good.

Try It

A. **Complete each sentence with I or me.**

1. "_____I_____ have a problem," said Mr. Angelo.
    I / me

2. Tess and _____I_____ learned that a big grocery was moving next door.
    I / me

3. "That store will put _____me_____ out of business," said Mr. Angelo.
    I / me

4. My friend and _____I_____ decided to help Mr. Angelo.
    I / me

B. **(5–8) Complete the sentences with I or me.**

I wrote ten reasons why people should keep shopping at Angelo's Grocery. Tess helped _____me_____ make copies of the list. Tess and _____I_____ posted the list around town. Some people asked Tess and _____me_____ questions. Tess and _____I_____ answered them.

C. Answer the questions. Use **I** and **me**.

9. What would you do if Angelo's Grocery were in your neighborhood? If Angelo's Grocery were in my neighborhood, _____

_____.

10. What kinds of neighborhood businesses are important to you and your friends? _____

_____

_____

D. (11–14) Now write at least four sentences telling why a neighborhood business is important to you and what you can do to support it. Use **I** and **me** in your sentences.

_____

_____

_____

_____

_____

Edit It

E. (15–20) Edit the letter. Fix six mistakes.

Dear Mayor Roberts:

My friends and I think you should not let a big chain grocery store come to our neighborhood. Our local grocer told my friends and I that he would go out of business. Me like shopping at Angelo's Grocery. My family and me will not shop anywhere else. Thank you for listening to I. My friends and me hope you can help us. Me think we have to support our small local businesses.

Sincerely,

Greg Yee

Proofreader's Marks

Change text:

My friends and ~~me~~ I
wanted to help. ∧

See all Proofreader's Marks on page ix.

94

44 Which Pronouns Refer to More Than One Person?

We, You, They, and Us, You, Them

With so many pronouns, how do you know which one to use in a sentence?

Pronouns	
Subject	**Object**
we	us
you	you
they	them

- Use a **subject pronoun** as the subject.

   My **friends and I** use the library a lot. **We** like to study there. _subject_

   The **city council members** had a meeting. **They** want to close the library. _subject_

- Use an **object pronoun** as the object of the verb.

   People in my neighborhood were upset. Closing the library will affect **them**. _object_

   We talked to the city council members. The council members listened to **us**. _object_
   subject

Try It

A. Complete each pair of sentences with a pronoun. Circle the word or words each pronoun refers to.

1. The (council members) explained the problem. _____They_____ said there was
   They / Them
   not enough money to run the library.

2. The library is important to (my neighbors and me). It gives _____us_____ a
   we / us
   place to read and study.

3. "(You and I) can keep the library open," said my friend. "_____We_____ can
   We / Us
   have a carwash to raise money."

4. We made (signs) advertising the carwash. Then we posted _____them_____
   they / them
   around town.

5. (My friends and I) collected buckets and sponges. A store gave _____us_____
   we / us
   soap.

B. (6–10) Complete the sentences using subject and object pronouns.

My brother and I stood on a corner with a sign. Lots of people driving by saw _____us_____. _____They_____ drove in to the carwash. Some people got out of their cars. Other people sat in _____them_____. My neighbors and I washed the cars. _____We_____ made them shine. The people paid _____us_____ ten dollars per car.

Write It

C. Answer the questions. Use subject and object pronouns in your sentences.

11. What do you think the neighbors did with the money they made? I think _____

_____

_____.

12. What do you think the city council members might say to the neighbors? _____

_____

_____

D. (13–15) Think about an issue in your school or community that people are trying to change. Write at least three sentences telling how you can participate. Use subject and object pronouns.

_____

_____

_____

_____

_____

45 Use Subject and Object Pronouns

Remember: Use a subject pronoun as the subject of a sentence. Use an object pronoun as the object of the verb.

Subject Pronouns	I	you	he	she	it	we	you	they
Object Pronouns	me	you	him	her	it	us	you	them

My friends and **I** have many heroes. **We** read about **them**. Helen Keller is one of our heroes. Do you know about **her**? **She** inspired many people. Cesar Chavez is another hero. **He** helped farm workers.

Try It

A. Rewrite each sentence, replacing the underlined word or words with the correct pronoun.

1. Susan B. Anthony is another hero of mine. _She is another hero of mine._

2. Susan B. Anthony wanted women to be able to vote. _Susan B. Anthony wanted them to be able to vote._

3. Women did not have the same rights as men. _They did not have the same rights as men._

4. Some men did not agree with Susan B. Anthony. _Some men did not agree with her._

5. My dad says that Susan B. Anthony is his hero, too. _He says that Susan B. Anthony is his hero, too._

B. (6–10) Complete the sentences with subject or object pronouns.

My friends and _____I_____ read about Mohandas Gandhi. _____We_____ think Gandhi was a great man. _____He_____ helped his countrymen and women overthrow British rule. Although _____they_____ suffered a lot, Gandhi encouraged _____them_____ to be nonviolent.

C. Answer the questions. Use subject and object pronouns.

11. Why do many people consider Martin Luther King, Jr. a hero? Many people _____

_____

_____.

12. How can an ordinary person be a hero? _____

_____

_____

D. (13–16) Think about one of your heroes. Write at least four sentences telling what this person has done that inspires you. Use subject and object pronouns.

_____

_____

_____

_____

_____

_____

Edit It

E. (17–20) Edit the paragraph. Fix four mistakes with subject and object pronouns.

Nelson Mandela is one of my heroes. He was born in a small
village in South Africa. ~~Him~~ He fought against unjust laws and
changed ~~they~~ them. The government sent ~~he~~ him to jail. But Mandela
continued to inspire people. ~~Them~~ They worked with Mandela to
change the laws. Mandela became South Africa's first black
president in 1994.

Proofreader's Marks

Change text:
                        us
Mandela gave ~~we~~ hope.

See all Proofreader's Marks
on page ix.

✔ Capitalize Proper Nouns

Capitalize specific days of the week and the names of months because they are **proper nouns**.

Common Nouns	Proper Nouns
day, night, today, year, summer, spring, autumn, winter	**Days of the Week:** Monday, Tuesday, Wednesday, Thursday, Friday, Saturday, Sunday
	Months: January, February, March, April, May, June, July, August, September, October, November, December

Try It

A. Use proofreader's marks to correct the capitalization error in each sentence.

1. Last tuesday in English class, we read "A Job for Valentín."

2. The story is about a disabled man who gets a job at the pool for the Summer.

3. The pool in our community will open at the end of may.

4. Last Year, I took swimming lessons every Saturday.

5. By the beginning of Autumn, hardly anyone goes swimming.

Proofreader's Marks

Capitalize:

school starts in August.

Do not capitalize:

The Spring of 2005 was unusually hot.

See all Proofreader's Marks on page ix.

B. (6–8) Pick one season and write at least three sentences describing activities you do during that season. Include days of the week and months. Sentences will vary.

_____

_____

_____

_____

✓ Punctuate Appositives and Nouns of Direct Address Correctly

- An **appositive** is a noun or pronoun placed next to another noun to identify it or to give more information about it. An **appositive phrase** is an appositive plus any words that modify it. You should usually use commas to set off an appositive or an appositive phrase.

    Teresa, **the teenage narrator of the story**, learns not to judge others by their appearance.

    A playful young boy, Pablito makes friends wherever he goes.

- Use commas to set off a **noun of direct address**, or the person to whom one is speaking.

    Valentín, let me show you how to do that.

    Yes, **Teresa**, I am coming to help you.

Try It

A. For each sentence, add or delete a comma.

9. Valentín, the main character of the story⌃looks after a little boy.

10. The boy's mother⌃Maricela, thinks Valentín is not smart.

11. Teresa⌃you will have a hard time teaching Valentín.

12. In the end, Valentín is the one⌀who teaches Teresa something new.

13. A caring person, Valentín helps save the young boy⌀from drowning.

Proofreader's Marks

Add comma:

"A Job for Valentín⌃" a story by
Judith Ortiz Cofer, is about a
mentally challenged man.

Delete:

The story is about a man⌀
who gets a job at the pool.

B. Rewrite each sentence by including the appositive phrase. Use commas correctly.

14. Pablito does not know how to swim. **(appositive phrase: the young boy in the story)**

    Pablito, the young boy in the story, does not know how to swim.

15. Valentín taught Teresa a valuable lesson. **(appositive phrase: a new employee)**

    Valentín, a new employee, taught Teresa a valuable lesson.

✔ **Check Sentences for Active Voice**

- In the **active voice**, the subject of a sentence performs the action.

    We read short stories every week.
    <small>subject action</small>

    Judith Ortiz Cofer wrote this story.
    <small>subject   action</small>

- In the **passive voice**, the person or thing performing the action is not the subject.

    Short stories are read by us every week.
    <small>subject   action   performer</small>

    This story was written by Judith Ortiz Cofer.
    <small>subject   action   performer</small>

- Avoid using the **passive voice** as much as possible in your writing. It can be awkward and hard to follow.

Try It

A. Decide whether each sentence uses the active voice or the passive voice. Then rewrite the sentence using the other voice.

16. He was spoken to loudly and slowly by her. ___passive; She spoke to him loudly___
and slowly.

17. We told Mrs. O'Brien that Pablito almost drowned. ___active; Mrs. O'Brien was told___
by us that Pablito almost drowned.

18. Permanent jobs at the pool were offered to us by her. ___passive; She offered us___
permanent jobs at the pool.

19. Mistakes about Valentín were made by Teresa. ___passive; Teresa made mistakes___
about Valentín.

20. Teresa showed Valentín how to pour drinks. ___active; Valentín was shown by___
Teresa how to pour drinks.

Name _____ Date _____

✔ Check for Consistency of Verb Tense

Check that you have used the correct verb tense and that you haven't switched from tense to tense. Change tense only if you talk about something that happened before or after the time you are writing about. The **present tense** of a verb tells about an action that is happening now. The **past tense** of a verb tells about an action that happened earlier or in the past.

> **Inconsistent verb tense:** By the end of the story, she **realized** (past tense) that Valentín **teaches** (present tense) her to stop judging others by their appearance.

> **Consistent verb tense:** By the end of the story, she **realized** (past tense) that Valentín **taught** (past tense) her to stop judging others by their appearance.

Try It

A. (21–26) Edit the story. Fix the six inconsistencies in verb tense.

> I remember what I learn^ed last summer when I volunteer^ed at the animal shelter. I worked with a girl named Sabina. She hardly ever talked to me unless it was to tell me what to do. I ~~think~~ thought she was rude. Then one day, one of the cats, Boomer, ran out of the shelter. Sabina talked to me about how upset she was. I told her that together we would find Boomer. Sure enough, we ~~find~~ found Boomer on the lawn, enjoying the sunny day. Sabina and I looked at each other and laughed. Now, we ~~were~~ are good friends, and we remembered the good times we had last summer.

Proofreader's Marks

Delete:

Yesterday, I ~~get~~ got a new dog.

Add text:
        is
He ∧ very playful.

B. (27–30) Write at least four sentences about a lesson you learned. Did something happen that changed your opinion about someone? Be sure to use the correct verb tense.

Sentences will vary.

_____

_____

_____

_____

_____

46 How Do I Show Possession?

One Way Is to Use a Possessive Noun.

- Use a **possessive noun** to show that someone owns, or possesses, something. Add **'s** if the possessive noun names one owner.

  Kathy reads the paper. **Kathy's** family reads *The City Daily.*

  Her **friend's** family reads *The Norwood Times.*

  Ted's teacher asks students to read articles aloud.

- A possessive noun can name more than one owner. Follow these rules:

  1. Add only an apostrophe if the plural noun ends in **-s**.

     The **students'** voices are expressive.

  2. Add **'s** if the plural noun does not end in **-s**.

     The **women's** magazine has a good health article.

Try It

A. Change the underlined words to a possessive noun. Write the possessive noun after each sentence.

1. The story about the politician was scandalous. _the politician's story_

2. The coverage by the media was excellent. _the media's coverage_

3. The interest of readers was high. _the readers' interest_

4. Articles by writers told both sides of the story. _writers' articles_

B. Rewrite each sentence to include a possessive noun. Possible responses:

5. The newspaper of my school is popular.
   My school's newspaper is popular.

6. Most articles by students teach me something new.
   Most students' articles teach me something new.

7. Sometimes the articles change the views of people.
   Sometimes the articles change people's views.

C. Answer the questions about reading the newspaper. Use a possessive noun correctly in each sentence.

8. Do you often agree with your friend's opinions about the news? _____

_____

9. Are your family's opinions changed by what they read in newspapers? _____

_____

10. Do you gain people's respect because of what you learn from reading? _____

_____

D. (11–14) Write at least four more sentences about how reading newspapers helps you. Use possessive nouns in your response.

_____

_____

_____

_____

_____

Edit It

E. (15–20) Edit the letter. Fix six mistakes with possessive nouns.

Dear Tanya,

Last night, Terry's parents came to our house for dinner. Terrys father was talking about a newspaper article at dinner. He disagreed with the authors views on poverty. My parents views were similar. After he expressed his opinion, I shared a few related facts from a newspaper article I had read. At first, I was scared to get involved in the adults discussion. But I talked anyway. You should have seen my parents faces. They were really proud of me!

Your friend,

Rachel

Proofreader's Marks
Delete:
My family's views ~~are~~ similar.
Add an apostrophe:
The girls mom listened.
Transpose:
We read the man article.
See all Proofreader's Marks on page ix.

47 What's a Possessive Adjective?

It's an Ownership Word.

- Use a **possessive adjective** to tell who has or owns something. Put the possessive adjective before the **noun**.

  Tim is a graphic artist. He is **my cousin**.
  His job interests me. **Our family** includes many artists.

- Match the possessive adjective to the **noun** or **pronoun** that it goes with.

  Tim told me about **his** friends at the studio.
  noun

  They are all artists. **Their** artwork is impressive.
  pronoun

Subject Pronoun	Possessive Adjective
I	my
you	your
he	his
she	her
it	its
we	our
they	their

Try It

A. Complete each sentence about careers. Use the correct form.

1. _____ *My* _____ brother Arnold is a firefighter.
   Me / My

2. I visited _____ *his* _____ firehouse because I want to be a firefighter, too.
   he / his

3. Other firefighters also brought _____ *their* _____ families to work.
   they / their

4. One firefighter said, "_____ *Your* _____ brother is very brave."
   You / Your

B. (5–8) Complete each sentence from the writer's point of view. Use possessive adjectives from the chart above.

I want to be a doctor, just like _____ *my* _____ mother. I know that

_____ *our* _____ city will need more doctors in the future. I asked my mother

about _____ *her* _____ education. I wondered if medical schools teach

_____ *their* _____ students different things today.

105

Write It

C. Answer these questions about careers. Use possessive adjectives.

9. Who do you talk to about his or her career? I talk with _____ about

_____ .

10. What kind of job does that person have? _____

_____

11. How do their views change your opinion of their job? _____

_____

D. (12–15) Write at least four more sentences about people you know whose careers interest you. Use possessive adjectives in each sentence.

_____

_____

_____

_____

Edit It

E. (16–20) Edit the journal entry. Fix the five mistakes in possessive adjectives.

December 3

For my career report, I visited cousin Vito

~~his~~
at ^he job. Later I told ^~~me~~ classmates all about
    ^ Our
~~his~~ ~~We~~ class has learned about many

careers, but Vito's job was awesome! He is an

oceanographer. When students heard that he
        their
often works underwater, ~~they~~^ jaws dropped.
                              her
They all had questions. Laura even said ^~~she~~

career plans changed after hearing my report.

Proofreader's Marks

Change text:
                his
That is ~~he~~ career.
           ^

See all Proofreader's Marks on page ix.

106

48 What Are the Possessive Pronouns?

Mine, Yours, His, Hers, Ours, and *Theirs*

Possessive Adjectives	my	your	his	her	our	their
Possessive Pronouns	mine	yours	his	hers	ours	theirs

Possessive adjectives
are used before a noun.

Possessive pronouns
stand alone.

My computer is fast.	This fast computer is **mine**.
That is **his** computer.	That computer is **his**.
There is **her** laptop.	That laptop is **hers**.
Our class meets on Thursdays.	The Thursday class is **ours**.
On Wednesdays, **their** class meets.	The Wednesday class is **theirs**.

Try It

A. Rewrite each sentence. Change the underlined words to the correct possessive pronoun.

1. I needed a computer, so my older sister let me use <u>her computer</u>. I needed a computer, so my older sister let me use hers.

2. One day she said the computer was <u>my computer</u> to keep. One day she said the computer was mine to keep.

3. Her company gave her one of <u>their computers</u>. Her company gave her one of theirs.

4. I told my little brother that the computer was <u>our computer</u> to share. I told my little brother that the computer was ours to share.

B. Complete each sentence with a possessive pronoun.

5. My neighbor works for a software company. That laptop computer is ____his____ .

6. He taught me to use software. Now, I create computer games that are all ____mine____ .

7. My friends like my games better than ____theirs____ .

8. I'd like to start a computer software business that is all ____mine____ .

9. My friend Julie wants to start a business that is all ____hers____ .

10. Maybe we can join together to create a software business that is all ____ours____ .

Write It

C. Answer the questions about computers and other technology. Use possessive pronouns.

11. Is the computer you work on yours or does it belong to your school? _____

_____

12. Do your friends depend more on their computers or their books to do homework? _____

_____

13. Do you have a calculator or other tools that you use to do your homework? _____

_____

14. Would you like to have a video camera that is all yours? Why? _____

_____

15. How could students use their computers to help them choose a college? _____

_____

D. (16–20) What special area of computer or other technology would you like to learn more about? Why? Write at least five sentences to explain. Use possessive pronouns.

_____

_____

_____

_____

_____

49 What's a Reflexive Pronoun?

It's a Word for the Same Person.

- Use a reflexive pronoun to talk about the same person or thing twice in a sentence. Reflexive pronouns end in -**self** or -**selves**.

  You know **yourself** and your study habits.

  Mary does not like to study by **herself**.

  Some students help **themselves** by studying in a group.

Reflexive Pronouns	
Singular	**Plural**
myself	ourselves
yourself	yourselves
himself,	themselves
herself, itself	

- Avoid these common mistakes with reflexive pronouns.

          himself
  1. Hashid told ~~hisself~~ that he would ace the test.

      themselves
  2. They get ~~theirselves~~ ready for the test.

Try It

A. Complete each sentence about joining a study group. Write the correct reflexive pronoun.

1. We must all prepare _____ourselves_____ for the big exam.

ourselves / ourself

2. Karen and Kim prepare _____themselves_____ by studying together.

theirselves / themselves

3. Kim told me, "Help _____yourself_____ by joining us."

yourselves / yourself

B. Draw a line from each noun or pronoun to the correct reflexive pronoun.

4. We surprised — "You can be proud of yourselves."

5. The teacher said, — ourselves by getting top grades.

6. Kim said that now — she has more confidence in herself.

7. Other students were mad — at themselves for not joining our group.

109

C. Answer the questions about studying. Use reflexive pronouns.

8. What happens when you study by yourself? When I study by _____.

9. How do your friends study? They study by _____.

10. How is studying alone different from studying with others? _____

_____.

D. (11–14) Write at least four sentences that tell how a study group can help you and other students. Use reflexive pronouns correctly.

_____

_____

_____

_____

Edit It

E. (15–20) Edit the letter. Fix the six mistakes in reflexive pronouns.

Dear Parents,

   Next week, students will take a final math exam. They

must prepare themselves for the test. Students can study by

themselves
theirselves, but study groups can help. You are welcome to set

                        yourselves   myself
up study groups by ourselves. I will also make me available for

                                              himself
private tutoring. Last year, one student gave himselves an extra

boost by joining two study groups. Many students later adopted

              themselves   ourselves
the same strategy for theirself. We can count ourselfs lucky

that our students are so hardworking.

Sincerely,

Ms. Juarez

Proofreader's Marks

Change text:

                    myself
I will study by ~~yourself~~.
                    ^

See all Proofreader's Marks
on page ix.

50 Show Possession

Remember: Use possessive words to show that someone owns something. A possessive adjective comes before a noun. A possessive pronoun stands alone.

Possessive Adjectives	my	your	his	her	its	our	your	their
Possessive Pronouns	mine	yours	his	hers		ours	yours	theirs

Try It

A. Complete each sentence. Write the correct possessive word.

1. My sister has seizures sometimes. This problem is not only _____ hers _____ .
   her / hers

2. Our family needs to be prepared. _____ My _____ reading helps me to
   Mine / My
   understand the disease.

3. _____ Its _____ warning signs are easy to miss. We must learn as much as
   Their / Its
   possible.

4. What I learn does not just have an effect on _____ her _____ health. It makes
   her / hers
   me much more aware of health issues.

5. My reading inspires me. I now understand that the responsibility for my own health is
   _____ mine _____ .
   my / mine

6. _____ Our _____ whole family is closer now. That is because we all work
   Our / Ours
   together to help my sister.

7. My sister is more confident. She feels the disease is not just _____ hers _____ .
   her / hers

B. **(8–12) Read the interview between two students for the school paper. Complete sentences with mine, hers, ours, yours, or theirs.**

Q. Whom have you helped with _____your_____ research?

A. My friend Jackie asked me to do research about diabetes on my computer. _____Hers_____ was broken. Diabetes was her problem, not _____mine_____, but I was happy to help.

Q. How did what you learn help Jackie?

A. I told Jackie about a girl with diabetes who posted her story online. Jackie said the girl had experiences similar to _____hers_____, which made her feel less alone. I also learned that exercise can help. My sister and I decided to walk with Jackie every day after school. Those walks not only made her body stronger, they strengthened _____ours_____, too.

Write It

C. **Answer the questions about your health knowledge. Use possessive adjectives and pronouns.**

13. What do you learn from friends or family with medical conditions? Explain. _____

_____

14. Have you helped friends or family to learn more about their conditions? How? _____

_____

15. What health issue concerns your family the most? _____

_____

16. Do you think people in general do enough research about their own health? _____

_____

D. **(17–20) Write at least four sentences about something you have learned recently that you use to stay healthy. Use possessive adjectives and pronouns.**

_____

_____

_____

_____

_____

51 What Kinds of Things Do Prepositions Show?

Location, Direction, and Time

Prepositions That Show Location: in, on top of, on, at, over, under, above, below, next to, beside, in front of, in back of, behind

- Use a preposition of **location** to tell where something is.

  Hector's mom keeps her old books **under** her bed.
  She keeps them **in** a big box.

Prepositions That Show Direction: into, throughout, up, down, through, across, to

- Use a preposition of **direction** to tell where something is going.

  Hector's sister Sonrisa reaches **into** the box and takes out a book.
  She and Hector look **through** the box to find something good to read.

Prepositions That Show Time: after, until, before, during

- Use a preposition of **time** to tell when something happens.

  Sonrisa finds a book **before** dinner. Hector finds his book **after** dinner.

Try It

A. Complete each sentence about reading a book. Add a preposition. Possible responses:

1. Hector starts to read the book _____on_____ the bus.

2. He sees that his mother has written her name _____in_____ the book.

3. Donna is sitting _____beside_____ Hector.

4. He holds the book _____near_____ her so she can see it, too.

B. Complete each sentence about reading a book. Choose the correct preposition.

5. The book is about a teenager in California _____during_____ the 1960s.

during / on

6. Donna tells Hector that she wants to go _____to_____ California.

at / to

7. Hector says he wants to live _____beside_____ the ocean someday.

beside / in

C. Answer the questions about reading. Use prepositions.

8. At what time of day do you usually read? _____

9. Where do you read? _____

10. What do you do with books after you read them? _____

11. Where do you get most of your books? _____

12. Do your friends or family recommend books to you after they have read them?_____

_____

D. (13–17) Write at least five sentences that tell about the books you most
enjoy reading. Use prepositions.

_____

_____

_____

_____

_____

Edit It

E. (18–25) Edit the letter. Fix the eight mistakes in prepositions.

Dear Uncle Bernie,

    Thank you for the great book. I loved reading something
you read during your teenage years. I also like science fiction
stories about life in other planets. I gave the book over my friend
Tim until school. He took it at his house. Don't worry, he will
return it during next Friday. I can't wait before your next visit! Will
that be above Saturday? I can return the book under your visit.

Your nephew,

Aaron

(edits marked above: on, to, after, before, to, before, until, before, during)

Proofreader's Marks
Change text: *after*
I read ~~before~~ dinner.
See all Proofreader's Marks on page ix.

114

Name _____ Date _____

52 How Do You Recognize a Prepositional Phrase?

Look for the Preposition.

- A **prepositional phrase** is a group of words that begins with a preposition and ends with a noun or pronoun. Use prepositional phrases to add information to your sentences.

  Victor walked **through the library**.
  noun

  He waved **to Felix** who sat **near the window**.
  noun   noun

- The **noun** at the end of a prepositional phrase is called the **object of the preposition**.

Try It

A. Add a prepositional phrase to tell more. Possible responses:

1. Victor found the book. He found the book _at the library_.

2. He read the story. He read the story _to his sister_.

3. Alex liked the book's setting. He liked the book's setting _in Africa_.

4. His sister liked the picture. She liked the picture _on the cover_.

5. Alex showed the book. He showed the book _to his friends_.

B. (6–11) Write a prepositional phrase to complete each sentence. You may use the same preposition more than once. Possible responses:

Victor finds an exciting new novel _at the library_. The story takes place _in Wyoming_. He shows it to Paco. Paco looks quickly _at the book_. He hands it back _to Victor_. He says that his family is going _to Madrid_. He wants to read a book about Spain. Victor puts the book back _into his backpack_.

115

C. Answer the questions below about your school library. Use prepositional phrases.

12. Where is the library in your school? _____

13. Are there many books on the shelves? _____

14. Where do you like to sit in the library? _____

15. Do you sit near your friends? _____

16. When do you go to the library? _____

D. (17–20) Write at least four sentences that describe what your school library looks like. Use prepositional phrases.

_____

_____

_____

_____

_____

Edit It

E. (21–25) Edit the letter. Fix the five mistakes in prepositional phrases.

Dear Lillie,

　　Yesterday, I found some old postcards in the garage. The
message under the back of one of the cards reads "Dear Mother,
last night we pitched our tents over the Mariposa Grove of Big
Trees in Yosemite Valley. One tree is 90 feet around!" Lillie, this
card is so exciting! It makes me want to go at Yosemite Valley
soon. Yosemite Valley is located over California. It will be fun to
camp for that tree.

Love,

Pat

Proofreader's Marks

Change text:
We stood over the tree. *inside*

See all Proofreader's Marks on page ix.

116

53 Can I Use a Pronoun After a Preposition?

Yes, Use an Object Pronoun.

- Use an **object pronoun** after a **preposition**.

  This is a good job **for me**.

  Dad discusses the interview **with me**.

Object Pronouns	
Singular	**Plural**
me	us
you	you
him, her, it	them

Try It

A. (1–5) Read this paragraph about preparing for a job interview. Add object pronouns.

Dad brought home a book about careers for _____ me _____. He showed me the part about gardening. He thought it would help me with my job interview. I read carefully through _____ it _____. Then Dad had me discuss the information with _____ him _____. The interview was in the morning. I felt well prepared for _____ it _____. Dad wished me luck. He said, "I'll be rooting for _____ you _____!"

B. Complete each sentence. Choose the correct object pronoun.

6. The interviewer had many questions for _____ me _____.

me / you

7. I thought I had good answers for _____ him _____.

it / him

8. He said, "I think you will fit right in with _____ us _____."

him / us

9. He added, "This is the perfect job for _____ you _____."

her / you

10. He said, "Welcome aboard" and smiled at _____ me _____.

me / you

Write It

C. Answer the questions about how reading can be helpful. Use object pronouns.

11. What helpful advice can you find in books? _____

12. Have you recommended useful books to a friend? _____

D. (13–15) Write at least three sentences that tell more about how reading books can help you. Use object pronouns.

_____

_____

_____

_____

Edit It

E. (16–20) Edit the journal entry. Fix the five mistakes with object pronouns.

March 14

It was a good day for me. It wasn't such a
good day for Tarik and Elicia. Everything
                                    them
seemed to go totally wrong for her. Our
teacher, Mrs. Sweeney, gave them good
advice about their upcoming job interviews.
                                    her
Unfortunately, Elicia did not listen to them.
She didn't get the job. Tarik read the book he
        her
got from you, but he started off late for the
interview. The interviewer looked at his watch.
He
Him saw that Tarik was ten minutes late. Tarik
wants to sell clothes in that store. I hope he
                    him
made that clear to me!

54 In a Prepositional Phrase, Where Does the Pronoun Go?

It Goes Last.

- A **prepositional phrase** starts with a preposition and ends with a noun or pronoun. Sometimes, it ends with both. Put the pronoun last.

    Cousin Marilyn showed a book **to my mom and me**.

    It was about living **in Sydney, Australia**. She loaned the book to my dad. She gave it **to him** last night.

- You can put a prepositional phrase at the start of the sentence to emphasize your idea.

    For her, moving to Australia is an important goal.

- Avoid these common mistakes in a prepositional phrase:

    1. Use **me**, not I:

                                                                me

    Not having Marilyn around would be sad for my parents and I.

                                                                        ∧

    2. Put **me** last:

                            my parents and me

    She is important to ~~me and my parents~~.

                                    ∧

Try It

A. Complete each sentence. Use the correct pronouns.

1. Marilyn said the move was an adventure for her family and _____ her _____.

                                                                                she / her

2. She added that she would always write to _____ her friends and us _____.

                                        us and her friends / her friends and us

3. For my parents and _____ me _____, thinking about Australia was exciting.

                                    me / I

4. My mom explained, "You are important to my husband and _____ me _____."

                                                                        me / I

5. However, they were very excited for _____ her _____.

                                                    she / her

6. For _____ us _____, Marilyn's move to Australia is sad.

                we / us

B. Complete each sentence. Use the correct pronouns.

7. Marilyn said we could visit her family and _____ her _____.

8. For my parents and _____ me _____, that was a wonderful invitation.

9. She thought our visit would be good for her and _____ us _____.

10. My father said, "That invitation means a lot to my wife and _____ me _____."

11. I said, "For Marilyn and _____ us _____, this visit will be very special."

Write It

C. Answer the questions about going places. Use pronouns correctly.

12. What place have you read about that you would like to see with your family? I have read about _____.

13. What would be fun for all of you to do in that place? _____
_____

14. Would moving to that place be a big change for you and your family? _____
_____

15. What effect might the move have on your friends and you? _____
_____

D. (16–20) Write at least five sentences that tell more about a place you would like to visit or live in with your family. Use pronouns correctly.

_____
_____
_____
_____
_____
_____

55 Use Pronouns in Prepositional Phrases

Remember: You can use prepositions to add details to your sentences. If you need a pronoun in a prepositional phrase, use an object pronoun.

Sentences with Prepositional Phrases

- I have books **about science, countries, and famous people**.
- Books have special importance **to me**.
- Many of the books are **for my sister and me**.
- My grandparents gave most of the books **to us** as presents.

Object Pronouns

Singular	Plural
me	us
you	you
him, her, it	them

Try It

A. Add a noun or an object pronoun to complete each prepositional phrase.

Possible responses:

1. I have one book about _____biology_____.

2. My grandfather is a biologist, and he gave the book to _____me_____.

3. The book about dancers is for _____my sister_____ and _____me_____.

4. My grandparents gave it to _____us_____ when we were little.

5. We used to create silly dance performances for _____them_____.

6. That book brings back fond memories for _____us_____ all.

B. Complete each sentence. Use the correct pronouns. Possible responses:

7. My grandparents always give nice gifts to _____her_____ and _____me_____.

8. For _____me_____, the books were the most special gifts.

9. When I was little, my grandmother made a cookbook for both of _____us_____.

10. We used it to bake a birthday cake for _____her_____.

C. Answer the questions about books. Use prepositional phrases with object pronouns.

11. For you, are books very important? _____

12. What kinds of books are special for you? _____

13. Did people give some of those books to you? Who? _____

14. Do the books bring back good memories for you? Explain. _____

15. What other kinds of books might be interesting for you to collect? _____

D. (16–20) Write at least five sentences that describe more about books that are important to you. Use prepositional phrases with object pronouns.

_____

_____

_____

_____

_____

_____

Edit It

E. (21–25) Edit the paragraph. Fix five mistakes in prepositional phrases.

My friend Emanuel says that books are important to him. I
                    us
agree! To we, the library is an exciting place. The range of
                                        Emanuel and me
subjects in the library is interesting for me and Emanuel. I
                                                    me
like the books on nature and animals. For I, these books are
the best. Emanuel prefers books on space exploration. To
him
he, space is exciting. I said, "Emanuel, here is a book about
taking animals on a space flight. This book would be great
        me
for you and I. Let's check it out!"

Proofreader's Marks

Change text:

Books are interesting to
you and I. me

See all Proofreader's Marks on page ix.

56 When Do You Use an Indefinite Pronoun?

When You Can't Be Specific

- When you are not talking about a specific person or thing, you can use an **indefinite pronoun**.

  Someone can teach you to read. **Anyone** here can help you.

- Some indefinite pronouns are always singular, so they need a **singular verb** that ends in **-s**.

  Everything seems to be ready. **Everybody** wants to learn.

Singular Indefinite Pronouns

another	each	everything	nothing
anybody	either	neither	somebody
anyone	everybody	nobody	someone
anything	everyone	no one	something

Try It

A. Complete each sentence about reading. Use the correct form of the verb.

1. My friends and I read about someone who _____ wants _____ to read.

want / wants

2. No one _____ knows _____ that Ken cannot read.

know / knows

3. Everything _____ is _____ difficult for him.

is / are

4. Ken hopes something _____ changes _____ soon.

change / changes

B. (5–9) Complete each sentence. Use indefinite pronouns from the chart above.

Possible responses:

My friends and I want to help _____ somebody _____ like Ken. We volunteer at the literacy center and do _____ something _____ to help. _____ Everyone _____ in our families can read. _____ Someone _____ who cannot read has fears. _____ Nothing _____ is more important than helping people read.

Write It

C. Answer the questions about literacy. Use indefinite pronouns correctly in each sentence.

10. Have you ever helped anyone learn to read? _____

11. How do you think someone who can't read might feel about literacy centers? _____

_____

D. (12–15) Write at least four sentences about how learning to read can help someone. Use indefinite pronouns in your response.

_____

_____

_____

_____

_____

Edit It

E. (16–20) Edit the journal entry. Fix five mistakes in indefinite pronouns.

October 17

Almost everyone I know volunteers at the
literacy center. They all want to help ~~nobody~~ someone
who cannot read. At the center, ~~everybody~~ no one
has to feel ashamed. The atmosphere is
supportive. ~~Nobody~~ Anybody can go to the center.
Once they learn to read, ~~anything~~ everything gets
easier. They realize how much fun reading
can be. Then ~~anyone~~ everyone feels better. I'm glad
that I'm able to help change people's lives.

Proofreader's Marks

Change text:

Everyone
~~Nobody~~ can learn to
read.

See all Proofreader's Marks on page ix.

57 Which Indefinite Pronouns Are Plural?

Both, Few, Many, and Several

- Use an **indefinite pronoun** when you are not talking about a specific person or thing.

  Several of the scientists in our city check our water supply.

  Many of the people in our town have been sick lately.

Plural Indefinite Pronouns	
both	many
few	several

- Some **indefinite pronouns** are always plural, so they need a **plural verb**.

  A **few** of our top scientists **talk** to the two government officials about the problem.

  Both of the officials **insist** that the situation is not serious.

Try It

A. Complete each sentence about water pollution. Use the correct form of the verb.

1. Many of the scientists who study the ocean _____ warn _____ that our water
   warn / warns
   supplies are polluted.

2. A few _____ study _____ the water in our local reservoir.
   study / studies

3. Both of the lakes in our city _____ are _____ also polluted.
   is / are

4. Several of our rivers _____ show _____ evidence of contamination.
   show / shows

5. Many of the people I know _____ avoid _____ eating fish from our lakes
   avoid / avoids
   altogether.

6. A few still _____ eat _____ fish from the rivers occasionally.
   eat / eats

B. Complete each sentence with a verb from the box.

agree	are	need	tell	volunteer

7. A few of the people in my city _____ are _____ really knowledgeable about water pollution.

8. They feel that both of our top scientists _____ need _____ to be part of the solution.

9. Both of my brothers _____ agree _____ that clean water is important.

10. Many of my friends ___ volunteer ___ on weekends to clean up the lake.

11. Several of them _____ tell _____ me I am welcome to join them.

Write It

C. Answer these questions about water pollution. Use the correct form of the verb.

12. Are several of your friends concerned about water pollution? _____

13. Do you think many of the students in your school know about the problem? _____

_____

14. What are a few of the steps people can take to stop water pollution? _____

_____

15. Do you think that adults and young people should help solve the problem? How can both of them work together? _____

_____

D. (16–20) Write at least five sentences about your views on water pollution. Use indefinite pronouns and verbs correctly in each sentence.

_____

_____

_____

_____

_____

58 Which Indefinite Pronouns Are Tricky?

The Ones That Can Be Singular or Plural

- The **indefinite pronouns** in the chart can be either singular or plural.

- The **prepositional phrase** after the pronoun shows whether the sentence talks about one thing or more than one thing. Use the correct **verb**.

Singular or Plural Indefinite Pronouns	
all	none
any	some
most	

Singular:	**Most** of the work **is** ahead of us.
Plural:	**Most** of the scientists **are** concerned.
Singular:	**Some** of the research **is** in progress.
Plural:	**Most** of the students **are** involved.
Singular:	**All** of the country **is** at risk.
Plural:	**All** of the experts **are** in agreement.

Try It

A. Complete each sentence about pollution. Use the correct form of the verb.

1. Some of the studies _____ reveal _____ the causes of air pollution.
   reveal / reveals

2. Most of the scientists _____ agree _____ that cars are part of the problem.
   agree / agrees

3. Any of the solutions _____ are _____ worth exploring.
   is / are

4. None of the work _____ is _____ wasted.
   is / are

5. Some of my neighbors _____ try _____ to do their part.
   try / tries

6. A few people _____ walk _____ to work instead of drive.
   walk / walks

B. Complete each sentence about car pollution with the correct form of a verb.

7. Most of our local pollution _____comes_____ from cars.

8. All of the cars _____need_____ to be more efficient.

9. Most of my neighbors _____want_____ cleaner air.

10. Some of my friends _____ride_____ mass transit.

Write It

C. Answer the questions about pollution. Use indefinite pronouns and verbs correctly.

11. Are most of your neighbors concerned about air pollution? _____

    _____

12. Do some of your friends drive cars? _____

    _____

13. Do all of the cars pollute the air? Explain? _____

    _____

14. Are any of the scientists in your city working to find solutions for the problem? _____

    _____

15. Do all of the scientists agree about the causes of pollution? _____

    _____

D. (16–20) What special area of air, water, or other pollution would you like to learn more about? Why? Write at least five sentences to explain. Use indefinite pronouns and verbs correctly.

_____

_____

_____

_____

_____

_____

59 What's an "Antecedent"?

It's the Word a Pronoun Refers To.

- A **pronoun** usually refers back to a noun. This noun is called the **antecedent**.

  Mr. Howard teaches me to play guitar. **He** is a good teacher.
  antecedent   pronoun

- A pronoun must **agree** with its antecedent. This means that the pronoun has to go with the noun it refers to.

  My **guitar** is new. **It** sounds beautiful.

  My **family** loves to hear me practice. **They** enjoy music.

Try It

A. **Identify the antecedent for the underlined pronoun. Add a sentence using the pronoun.**
Sentences will vary.

1. Mr. Harrison tells me to practice. <u>He</u> says that practice helps me learn. ___antecedent: Mr. Harrison; He also practices daily.

2. My brother and I play music together. <u>We</u> both love to play. ___antecedent: My brother and I; We both study guitar with Mr. Harrison.

3. Music is my favorite activity. <u>It</u> is important to me. ___antecedent: Music; It also makes me feel happy.

4. My cousins also play music. <u>They</u> play piano and violin. ___antecedent: My cousins; They are very talented.

B. **Add a sentence to each item to continue the idea of the first sentence. Use the correct pronoun for each underlined antecedent.** Possible responses:

5. <u>My mother</u> likes Mr. Harrison. ___She thinks he is a good musician.

6. <u>My teacher</u> has many students. ___He loves to teach.

7. <u>My brother and I</u> want to teach music someday, too. ___We work hard to improve.

C. Answer the questions about learning a skill. Include pronouns and the correct antecedents.

8. What skill would you like to learn? I would like to _____.

9. Who would you like to study with? _____

10. Would you like to use this skill in your career? Explain. _____

D. (11–14) Write at least four sentences about someone who is skilled in your area of interest. Use pronouns and antecedents correctly.

_____

_____

_____

_____

_____

Edit It

E. (15–20) Edit the journal entry. Fix the six mistakes in pronouns.

November 14

Aunt Roberta let me paint with her today. ~~We~~ She is a really fine artist. My aunt shows her paintings in a gallery. ~~He~~ It is a big space in a fancy building. Many people buy her paintings. ~~She~~ They love the way she paints landscapes. Her paintings are large. ~~It~~ They are sometimes more than four feet wide! Painting is the career I want to have. ~~They~~ It is not always easy, but it is what I love. Aunt Roberta and my cousin Arnie are both artists. ~~He~~ They both said they will teach me to paint.

Proofreader's Marks

Change text:

Arnie paints. ~~They~~ He is an artist.

See all Proofreader's Marks on page ix.

60 Use the Correct Pronoun

Remember: When you use a pronoun, be sure it fits correctly into the sentence. Also be sure it goes with the noun it refers to.

- Use a **subject pronoun** in the subject of a sentence. Use an **object pronoun** after the verb or after a preposition.

  Larry talks to **Karen**. **He** tells **her** how he reached his career goal.

  His **friends** chose the same **career**. **They** love **it**.

- All **pronouns** must agree with the **noun** they refer to. This noun is called the antecedent.
  1. If the noun names a male, use **he** or **him**.
  2. If the noun names a female, use **she** or **her**.
  3. If a noun names one thing, use **it** or **it**.
  4. If a noun names "more than one," use **they** or **them**.

Try It

A. Complete each sentence. Write the correct pronouns.

1. Larry has a good job. _____ He _____ worked hard to get it.
   He / They

2. Larry told his sister how he reached his goal. He spent years preparing for
   _____ it _____ .
   it / them

3. Students in high school must take science. They must be good at
   _____ it _____ .
   it / them

4. Teens should study biology. They need a strong background in _____ it _____ .
   it / them

5. Hospitals are happy to have young volunteers. They can offer good medical experience to
   _____ them _____ .
   it / them

B. **(6–9) Complete each sentence. Use the correct subject and object pronouns.**

Larry worked for Dr. Lehrer in high school. _____He_____ learned a lot from _____him_____. After his junior year, Larry attended a special summer program. _____It_____ was a medical school program for teens. The program helped _____them_____ see if they might want to become doctors.

Write It

C. **Answer the questions about career goals. Use subject and object pronouns correctly.**

10. Who do you know who has reached an important career goal? _____

11. What types of things did that person have to learn in order to reach that goal? _____

_____

12. What steps did they take to prepare for their career? _____

_____

D. **(13–16) Write at least four sentences about a career that interests you. Discuss at least two things you would have to learn to reach that goal. Use subject and object pronouns correctly.**

_____

_____

_____

Edit It

E. **(17–20) Edit the letter. Fix the five mistakes with pronouns.**

Dear Dr. Larry Harris,

    I am delighted to offer you a position. Your job begins on September 3rd. ~~They~~ It will involve three main responsibilities. ~~It~~ They are examination, diagnosis, and treatment. Mr. Harris is the head of your department. ~~Him~~ He will be happy to answer questions. You will receive pension benefits. ~~Them~~ They begin on your first day.

Sincerely,

Dr. Julian Ottavio

Proofreader's Marks
Change text:
He ⌄ ~~Him~~ is a doctor. ⌃
See all Proofreader's Marks on page ix.

132

✔ Capitalize the Titles of Publications

- Capitalize all main words in the titles of publications, such as books, magazines, newspapers, and articles.

  Book: *Successful Television Writing*

  Magazine: *Electronic House*

  Newspaper: *USA Today*

  Article: "Bonus Features Aid TV DVD Craze"

- Do not capitalize **a**, **on**, **the**, or **of** unless it is the first word in the title.

  Television: Technology and Cultural Form

  The New York Times

Try It

A. Use proofreader's marks to correct the capitalization error in each sentence.

1. My uncle reads *The Wall street Journal*.

2. I am halfway through *Fifty Years Of Television*.

3. I e-mailed you an article. It's called "Will Reality TV survive?"

B. Answer each question. Be sure to capitalize titles correctly.
Sentences will vary.

4. What is the name of your school newspaper?

_____

5. What textbook do you use in your science class?

_____

6. What is the name of your favorite magazine?

_____

Proofreader's Marks
Capitalize: He reads the *Chicago sun-times*.
Do not capitalize: My favorite book is *Gone With The Wind*.
See all Proofreader's Marks on page ix.

✓ Use Parentheses Correctly

- Use **parentheses** to set off a sentence or phrase that interrupts an idea. This includes citations in research reports.

  Americans (according to ACNielsen) watch more than four hours of TV each day. That means they watch twenty-eight hours per week (Herr 8).

- Place end punctuation after the end parenthesis of a citation or interrupting phrase.

  American children spend 1,500 hours per year watching TV (compared with 900 hours per year attending school).

  They also see approximately 30,000 TV commercials per year (Hartung 23).

- Place the end quotation mark for a direct quotation before the citation in parentheses.

  In years to come, "Americans will spend half their lives watching TV, going online, listening to music, and reading" (Kornblum A5).

Try It

A. (7–10) Fix the four errors in punctuation. Use proofreader's marks.

Most people think it began with *Survivor*, but reality TV has actually been around for nearly as long as television itself (late 1930s). The phenomenon began in 1948 with a show called *Candid Camera* (Jacobs 52). Created and hosted by Allen Funt, the show featured ordinary Americans who found themselves in perplexing situations, which were set up by the show's producers. These scenarios usually involved trick props (a desk with drawers that randomly pop open, for example) or some other type of prank. In one episode, Funt "pretended to be an airport security person and instructed passengers to go down the conveyor belt through a fake X-ray machine" (Jacobs 146)". The show's victims would be confused and sometimes angry until they heard the famous tag line: "Smile! You're on Candid Camera!"

Proofreader's Marks

Add parentheses:

The first television was built in 1927 (Jones 15).

Add quotation marks:

"I saw you on TV last night," she said.

Delete:

I like ~~like~~ reality TV.

✓ Use Consistent Verb Tense

- Do not change tenses in a paragraph or essay unless you are talking about something that happened before or after the time that you are writing about.

  Right now, I **want** to watch my favorite TV show. I **taped** it last night because I was busy studying for a test.

- In general, use the **past tense** to tell a story about historical events.

  The first television broadcast **appeared** in London in 1938.

  Once upon a time, there **lived** a family who **didn't own** a television set. They **had** conversations with each other and **read** books to entertain themselves.

- Use the **present tense** to talk about statistics; literary, film, and television works; actions that happen on a regular basis; and your own ideas.

  Ninety-nine percent of households in the United States **have** at least one television set.

  Jayden **watches** one hour of television every night.

  I **believe** that Americans **need** to watch less television.

Try It

A. (11–15) Fix the five inconsistencies in verb tense. Use proofreader's marks.

In the early 1950s, the most popular form of television comedy was the comedy-variety show, which ~~transfers~~ transferred easily to television from radio. This type of show ~~is~~ was usually hosted by a celebrity. One of the most famous early comedy-variety shows was *The Texaco Star Theater* with Milton Berle as host.

In the late 1950s, however, a new form of television comedy became popular—the situation comedy, or sitcom. This form really took off with the production of *I Love Lucy*, starring Lucille Ball and Desi Arnaz. The show revolutionized the television industry: It ~~is~~ was the first program filmed in California instead of New York; it ~~is~~ was the first program filmed with the three-camera technique; and, it ~~sets~~ set the basic plotline for situation comedies for years to come.

Proofreader's Marks

Change text:
                    are
What ~~were~~ you watching?

✓Make Pronouns Agree with Their Antecedents

- A **pronoun** usually refers back to a noun. This noun is called the **antecedent**.

  Where is the **remote**? Isn't **it** on the coffee table?

  antecedent   pronoun

- A pronoun must **agree** with its antecedent. It must match the noun it refers to in gender (male or female) and number (singular or plural).

  Jorge still can't find the remote. **He** has looked everywhere.

  Ask **Rachel and Vanessa**. **They** were watching TV this afternoon.

Try It

A. **(16–21) Complete the story by adding the correct pronouns. Draw an arrow from each pronoun to its antecedent.**

Eugene McDonald was the founder of Zenith Electronics Corporation. _____He_____

wanted to give people a way to control their TVs from their couches. _____He_____

met with Zenith's engineers and asked _____them_____ to come up with an idea.

_____They_____ created a device called the Lazy Bones. _____It_____ was

connected to the TV by a cable. _____It_____ was very awkward to use.

B. **(22–25) Edit the report. Fix the four pronouns. Use proofreader's marks.**

He
McDonald wanted something better. It went back to the engineers
them
and told him to create a remote without wires. One engineer,
Eugene Polley, created a remote that used a light beam to control
It
the TV. She became known as the Flashmatic. Unfortunately, the
It
TV didn't just respond to the Flashmatic. They also responded to
sunlight, which caused the TV to turn on and off by itself.

Proofreader's Marks

Change text: it
Can you fix him?

61 What Are Adjectives?

They Are Describing Words.

- You can describe people, places, or things with **adjectives**. They answer the question: What is it like?

- Use adjectives to describe

  1. how something looks: **strange, bumpy, threatening, gigantic**

  2. how something sounds: **loud, shrill, metallic**

  3. how something feels, tastes, or smells: **rough, fresh, salty**

  4. a person's mood: **tired, optimistic, sad, angry**

- Adjectives help the reader visualize what you are writing about. The **ominous** clouds blew across the already **darkening** sky. **Roaring** thunder was preceded by **sharp** daggers of lightning.

Try It

A. Add excitement to the story about the unexpected storm. Use adjectives from the box.
Possible responses:

explosive	frightened	horrendous	howling	sudden

1. The ___horrendous___ storm was unexpected.

2. I heard an ___explosive___ noise, and the lights went out.

3. The ___sudden___ silence disturbed me.

4. Then the ___howling___ wind began to screech outside my windows.

5. My ___frightened___ dogs hid under the bed.

B. Now think of your own adjectives. Write them to complete the sentences. Possible responses:

6. Usually, I don't mind storms, but this ___unexpected___ storm was scaring me.

7. I heard every ___creaking___ sound and jumped.

8. Was an ___uninvited___ stranger in the house with me?

C. Answer the questions to tell about a time when something unexpected happened when you were home alone. Use at least one adjective in each answer.

9. What happened? I _____

_____.

10. Were you scared? Why? _____

_____

11. How did you handle the situation? _____

_____

D. (12–15) Write at least four sentences to tell about a time the power went out unexpectedly during a storm. Use adjectives in your sentences.

_____

_____

_____

_____

_____

Edit It

E. (16–20) Improve the journal entry. Add five adjectives. Possible responses:

	Proofreader's Marks
September 30	**Add text:**
Tonight, a scary thing happened to me. I was	There was a _∧ wind. *howling*
home all alone when we had a ^{raging}_∧ storm. My house	See all Proofreader's Marks on page ix.
lost power. I heard ^{thunderous}_∧ noises all evening long.	
The only light I had was the ^{dim}_∧ light from my	
flashlight. My ^{frightened}_∧ dogs just hid under the bed.	
I sat alone in the ^{dark}_∧ house until my parents came	
home.	

138

62 Where Do Adjectives Appear in a Sentence?

Usually Before the Noun

- Often the **adjective** comes before the **noun** you are describing.
  The **dark house** made **creaky noises**.
  The **pounding rain** broke the **eerie silence**.

- If two adjectives both describe the noun, separate them with a comma (,).
  Cold, clammy air filled the house.
  I sat and hoped that the **furious, windy rain** would soon end.

Try It

A. Write adjectives to complete the sentences. Possible responses:

1. Besides scaring me, this storm was causing another ____unexpected____ problem.

2. I had a ____huge____, ____unfinished____ history paper due the next day.

3. I was sitting in my ____silent____ house in ____total____ darkness, though.

4. My normally ____humming____ computer was quiet.

5. I worried about the ____big____, ____fat____ zero I was going to get on my paper.

B. (6–12) Write adjectives to complete the paragraph. Possible responses:

Finally, at around 10 o'clock, the ____whistling____ wind died down. The ____deafening____, ____pounding____ rain stopped. A short while later, my ____wary____ dogs ventured out from under the bed! But best of all, the lights came on. I spent a very ____long____ night completing my ____dreaded____ homework, and I learned not to put things off until the ____last____ moment.

C. Complete each sentence to describe a storm. Use adjectives.

13. One _____ day, _____.

14. The _____, _____ sky _____.

15. My _____, _____ family and I _____
_____.

16. The storm was like a _____.

D. (17–20) Write at least four sentences about a time when you put off homework and then something unexpected happened. Use adjectives in each sentence.

_____

_____

_____

_____

_____

Edit It

E. (21–25) Improve the news article. Add five adjectives.   Possible responses:

Devastating Storm Blacks Out Region

The whole region suffered the effects of last night's ^powerful storm.
Houses and businesses all over the state lost power. The ^howling winds
caused ^huge trees to topple and power lines to fall. Today, some
^lucky people have their power back. Many other people are still sitting
in the ^gloomy dark.

Proofreader's Marks
Add text:
Many ^unfortunate people are still without power.
See all Proofreader's Marks on page ix.

63 How Do You Use a Predicate Adjective?

After a Form of the Verb *Be*

- Most of the time, **adjectives** come before **nouns**.
  A **scary** **event** happened to me yesterday.

- If the verb is a form of **be**, you can put the adjective after the verb. The forms of **be** are **am**, **is**, **are**, **was**, and **were**.
  The **event** was **scary**. At first, **I** was **worried**.

- If you use two predicate adjectives, join them with **and**, **but**, or **or**.
  Yesterday, I was **shocked** **and** **nervous**. Today, I am **anxious** **but** **excited**.
  Are you **jittery** **or** **relaxed** when you perform?

Try It

A. Use adjectives from the box to complete the sentences. Possible responses:

fantastic	horrified	ready	sick	surprised	thrilled

1. Yesterday, I was ____surprised____ to get a call from the play's director.

2. She told me that the lead actor was ____sick____.

3. She asked me, "Are you ____ready____ to stand in for him?"

4. I was ____horrified____ but ____thrilled____.

5. This opportunity was ____fantastic____ for me.

B. Now think of your own adjectives. Write them to complete the sentences. Possible responses:

6. I am ____anxious____ and ____nervous____ on opening night.

7. I am not ____afraid____, though.

8. I am ____comfortable____ and ____ready____ with my lines.

9. It is ____scary____ to get up on stage.

10. On the other hand, the experience is ____wonderful____ and ____rewarding____.

C. Complete each sentence to tell about a time when you had to suddenly prepare for an unexpected event. Use predicate adjectives.

11. I was _____ and _____ when _____

_____.

12. The experience was _____ because _____

_____.

13. Now I am _____ that it happened because _____

_____.

D. (14–16) Write at least three sentences about something unexpected that could happen during a school performance or sports event. Use predicate adjectives.

_____

_____

_____

_____

_____

Edit It

E. (17–20) Edit the play review for the school newspaper. Add four predicate adjectives.

Last night's play was both scary and terrific. The actors were. fantastic
The lead actor had only three days to learn the role. This
reviewer thinks he did an incredible job. His acting was. superb My
recommendation is that you see this play before closing night.
I am glad that I did. You will find that the play is very. suspenseful

Proofreader's Marks
Add text: happy I was to be in the play.
See all Proofreader's Marks on page ix.

64 Why Do You Use a Demonstrative Adjective?

To Point Something Out

- A **demonstrative adjective** signals where something is—either near or far.

- Use **this** and **these** for something near you.
  This play has fantastic props.
  I helped make **these props** here.

- Use **that** and **those** for something far from you.
  Did you like **that prop** over there at the back of the stage?
  I think **those props** over there are scary.

Demonstrative Adjectives	
Singular	**Plural**
this	these
that	those

Try It

A. Write the correct demonstrative adjective to complete each sentence.

1. The audience really enjoyed _____ this _____ play.

this / these

2. _____ That _____ actor on the other side of the room was so scary.

This / That

3. I jumped out of my seat when _____ those _____ loud noises blared.

that / those

4. I wasn't expecting _____ that _____ bright light display, either.

that / those

5. Both of _____ those _____ things helped build up the suspense.

that / those

6. The surprise caused by _____ these _____ special effects was incredible.

this / these

7. Everyone in _____ this _____ audience screamed.

this / that

8. I think _____ these _____ special effects in this play are the best ever!

these / those

143

B. Fix the demonstrative adjective in each sentence.

    9. The main character in ~~these~~ this play turns into a monster.

  10. In ~~this~~ these three acts right here, he is a man.

  11. Then he puts on ~~these~~ that scary costume over there.

  12. ~~These~~ Those sharp fangs that you see over there startled me.

  13. ~~This~~ These special effects here built up suspense, too.

  14. All of ~~these~~ those costumes and special effects that we saw earlier made the play more frightening.

Write It

C. Answer the questions about your favorite special effects from a movie you have seen. Use demonstrative adjectives.

  15. Were the special effects scary? _____

_____

  16. How would you describe the special effects? _____

_____

  17. Why did you like them? _____

_____

D. (18–20) Write at least three sentences about a scary scene in a movie you have seen. Use demonstrative adjectives.

_____

_____

_____

_____

_____

65 Use Adjectives to Elaborate

Remember: Use adjectives to add interesting, lively details to your writing. Adjectives help readers see, hear, touch, smell, and taste.

See	Hear	Touch	Smell	Taste
enormous	metallic	icy	burnt	salty
red	shrill	rough	smoky	sour
shiny	whistling	sticky	sweet	spicy

       secondhand   deserted   spooky

Oh, no! My car just died on the ~~unused~~ highway near the ~~dark~~ woods.
                   ^   ^   ^

Try It

A. Write adjectives to make the sentences more interesting. Possible responses:

1. My friends and I were _____ jittery _____ and _____ jumpy _____ as we waited for help to arrive.

2. We sat in the _____ frigid _____ darkness with only the _____ glowing _____ moon for light.

3. One friend was telling us about the _____ gigantic _____ bear that had wandered into her yard.

4. All of a sudden, I heard _____ thumping _____ noises coming from the woods.

5. Were those _____ scary _____, _____ threatening _____ noises a bear?

B. (6–12) Write adjectives to make the paragraph more interesting. Possible responses:

My friend kept on telling her story. Now I was really _____ scared _____! What would we do if a _____ fierce _____, _____ hungry _____ bear came out of the woods? My _____ overactive _____ imagination went to work. I thought of all the _____ wild _____ animals stalking us, and I headed back to the _____ abandoned _____ car. I felt safer there. I was really _____ happy _____ to see my parents and the tow truck finally arrive.

C. Complete each sentence to tell about the woods at night. What unexpected things might you see or hear? Use interesting adjectives.

13. If I were stranded in the woods at night, I might see _____

_____.

14. I might hear _____.

15. I hope I would not see _____.

16. The scariest thing would be _____.

D. (17–20) Write at least four sentences to tell about a time when you were scared. Use at least one interesting adjective in each sentence.

_____

_____

_____

_____

_____

E. (21–25) Improve the letter. Change five adjectives to make them more interesting. Possible responses:

Dear Grandma,

You wouldn't believe what happened to me last night! My car died out near Wild Woods Park. It was a ~~good~~ lucky thing that I had my cell phone. I called Mom right away. Mom is always so ~~nice~~ helpful. She called the tow truck. My friend Maria told a ~~bad~~ frightening story about a bear. Then, I started to hear ~~noisy~~ crunching sounds. I thought it was a ~~big~~ ferocious bear. It turned out to be the wind blowing in the tree branches. I was relieved when Mom and the tow truck arrived.

Love,

Amanda

Proofreader's Marks
Change text: spooky The noises were ~~bad~~.
See all Proofreader's Marks on page ix.

66 Can You Use an Adjective to Make a Comparison?

Yes, But You Have to Change the Adjective.

- Use a **comparative adjective** to compare two people, places, or things.

  My basketball team is **strong**, but the other team is **stronger**.
  That team is **more athletic** than ours.

- There are two ways to turn an adjective into a comparative adjective:

1. If the adjective is short, add **-er**. If it ends in **y**, change the **y** to **i** before you add **-er**.	long old scary **longer** **older** **scarier**
2. If the adjective is long, use **more** before the adjective.	unexpected frightening **more unexpected** **more frightening**

- If an adjective is medium length, use the form that is easier to say:

  friendly   **nervous**

  friendlier or **more friendly**   **more nervous**

Try It

A. Complete each sentence about the opposing basketball team. Write the comparative form of the adjective.

1. Our players are **tall**, but the other players are _____ taller _____.

2. We can be **intimidating**, but they are even _____ more intimidating _____.

3. Our guards are **fast**, but their guards are _____ faster _____.

4. Our shooting percentage is **high**, but theirs is _____ higher _____.

5. Usually I am **anxious** before the game, but this time I am _____ more anxious _____ than ever.

6. My coach is **fearful** that we will get crushed, but I am even _____ more fearful _____.

B. Complete each sentence. Write the correct form of the adjective in parentheses.

7. The buzzer is especially _____loud_____ at the beginning of the game. **(loud)**

8. Their center is _____quicker_____ than ours, and he taps the jump ball to his player. **(quick)**

9. Their second shot is ____more accurate____ than their first shot. **(accurate)**

10. They score a _____fast_____ two points. **(fast)**

11. Our defense is ___more aggressive___ than it should be, and we foul them on the shot. **(aggressive)**

12. They are up three to nothing, and we feel _____gloomier_____ now than we did before the game. **(gloomy)**

Write It

C. Compare two competing athletes, political candidates, or other celebrities. Use at least one comparative adjective in each sentence.

13. _____ is _____, but _____ is _____.

14. Right now, _____ is _____ than _____.

15. In the end, _____ will be _____ than _____.

16. I am _____ than I was _____.

D. (17–20) Write at least four sentences to compare your favorite sports team to another. Use comparative adjectives in your sentences.

_____

_____

_____

_____

_____

67 Can an Adjective Compare More Than Two Things?

Yes, But You Have to Use a Different Form.

- A **superlative adjective** compares three or more people, places, or things. You can turn an adjective into a superlative adjective:

1. Add **-est** to a short adjective.	This is **the toughest** team we've ever played.
2. Use **most** before a long adjective.	It is **the most difficult** game ever.

- Adjectives have different forms. Use the form that fits your purpose.

To Describe 1 Thing	dark	competitive
To Compare 2 Things	darker	more competitive
To Compare 3 or More Things	darkest	most competitive

- Never use **more** and **-er** together. Never use **most** and **-est** together.

  It is the ~~most~~ longest game ever.

Try It

A. Write the correct adjective to complete each sentence about how the team's fear becomes a reality.

1. This game is turning into the _____ most humiliating _____ game my team
   more humiliating / most humiliating
   has ever played.

2. By halftime, their lead is even _____ greater _____ than it was after
   greater / greatest
   the first quarter.

3. I feel the _____ most hopeless _____ feelings in the world.
   hopelessest / most hopeless

4. At halftime, our coach is _____ wonderful _____, though.
   wonderful / more wonderful

5. He thinks that this is the _____ strongest _____ team we've ever played.
   strongest / most strongest

B. Edit the sentences. Fix the adjectives.

6. Well, my most ~~horriblest~~ *horrible* fears have come true.

7. We have had our ~~more~~ *most* terrible loss ever.

8. I am ~~happiest~~ *happier* after the game than I was before it, though.

9. I played my ~~most~~ hardest game ever.

10–11. I learned that sometimes the *most* difficult losses of all teach us the ~~importantest~~ *most important* lessons.

12. I feel ~~unhappier~~ *unhappy* that we lost but pleased that we lost by only 10 points. It could have been worse.

Write It

C. Write three new facts about the game. Use superlative adjectives in each sentence.

13. I felt the _____ of all when _____ .

14. The _____ player of all the players on the other team was _____
_____ .

15. The _____ moment of all the moments in the game was when _____
_____ .

D. (16–20) Write an article for the school newspaper. Use at least five sentences to tell about the game. Include a comparative or superlative adjective in each sentence.

_____

_____

_____

_____

_____

_____

68 Which Adjectives Are Irregular?

Good, Bad, Many, Much, and Little

- These adjectives have special forms.

To Describe 1 Thing	good	bad	many	much	little
To Compare 2 Things	better	worse	more	more	less
To Compare 3 or More Things	best	worst	most	most	least

I have a **little** gas in my car.

Fred has **less** gas in his car than I have in mine.

Walter has the **least** gas of all.

Try It

A. Write the correct adjective to complete each sentence.

1. I had a _____ bad _____ feeling about driving down the deserted road.
   bad / worst

2. Walter had an even _____ worse _____ feeling than I did.
   worse / worst

3. Fred thought that it was the _____ best _____ idea of all.
   better / best

4. So I used the _____ worst _____ judgment I've ever used.
   worse / worst

5. I experienced _____ more _____ fear then than I ever did before.
   more / most

B. Now write adjectives from the chart above to complete the sentences. Possible responses:

6. My _____ worst _____ fears of all came true.

7. Despite the _____ best _____ planning in the world, my car ran out of gas.

8. It was a _____ good _____ thing that I had my cell phone.

9. In what seemed like the _____ most _____ minutes ever, my mom arrived with gas.

Write It

C. Complete the sentences to tell about when one of your fears came true. Use adjectives from the chart.

10. My _____ fear ever came true when _____

_____.

11. That experience was _____ than I thought because _____

_____.

12. Now I have the _____ memories of all because _____

_____.

D. (13–16) Write at least four sentences about fears you hope will not come true. Use adjectives from the chart on page 151.

_____

_____

_____

_____

Edit It

E. (17–20) Edit the journal entry. Fix the four incorrect adjectives.

January 15

Last night was the worst night of my life.
I made a ~~worst~~ *bad* decision to drive my car
with very ~~least~~ *little* gas in it. It turned out to
be a bad decision ~~than~~ *worse* I thought. The ~~better~~ *best*
thing of all the things that happened was
that Mom didn't get mad at me. She said
that she'd done some silly things when she
was a teenager, too.

Proofreader's Marks

Change text:
I had ~~most~~ *more* problems last
night than I expected.

See all Proofreader's Marks
on page ix.

(69) When Do You Use an Indefinite Adjective?

When You Can't Be Specific

- If you are not sure of the exact number or amount of something, use an **indefinite adjective**.

  The ocean has **many** sharks. **Several** kinds of sharks swim in warm water.
  Some areas have **a lot of** sharks, and **some** areas have **a few** sharks.

- Do you know which adjective to use?

These adjectives go before a noun you can count, like **sharks**:		These adjectives go before a noun you can't count, like **water**:	
many sharks	**a lot of** sharks	**much** water	**a lot of** water
a few sharks	**several** sharks	**a little** water	**not much** water
some sharks	**no** sharks	**some** water	**no** water

Try It

A. Complete each sentence with an indefinite adjective from the chart. More than one answer is possible. Possible responses:

1. I have _____a lot of_____ fear when I swim in the ocean.

2. That's because I have seen _____several_____ movies about sharks.

3. In _____a lot of_____ movies, people get hurt.

4. I have _____a little_____ fear when I swim in lakes.

5. _____No_____ sharks swim in lakes around here.

B. (6–12) Write adjectives from the chart to complete the paragraph. More than one answer is possible. Possible responses:

Yesterday, I was swimming _____a few_____ laps in the ocean. I was proud of

myself for overcoming _____many_____ fears. Suddenly, I felt _____a lot of_____

fear because I saw _____many_____ shark fins! My worst fears were coming

true! I felt _____a lot of_____ panic. Then I noticed that _____no_____ fins were

moving. The "fins" were _____several_____ rocks sticking up in the water.

C. Describe an ocean or a lake. Use indefinite adjectives from the chart.

13. I see _____

_____.

14. I hear _____

_____.

15. I enjoy _____

_____.

16. I fear _____

_____.

D. (17–20) Write at least four sentences about an experience you have had while you were swimming. Use indefinite adjectives.

_____

_____

_____

_____

_____

Edit It

E. (21–25) Edit the report about sharks. Fix the five incorrect indefinite adjectives. There is more than one correct answer. Possible responses:

There are many kinds of sharks. ~~A little~~ Some sharks are dangerous.
The great white shark is dangerous. ~~Much~~ Several / A lot of sharks are harmless.
The whale shark is harmless but huge. ~~Much~~ A few sharks have sharp
teeth and eat fish. ~~A little~~ A little sharks, like the megamouth, eat
plankton. ~~Much~~ A little knowledge goes a long way in understanding
sharks!

Proofreader's Marks

Change text:
~~Much~~ Many sharks live in the
ocean.

See all Proofreader's Marks
on page ix.

70 Use Adjectives Correctly

Remember: You can use adjectives to describe or compare people, places, or things.

To Describe 1 Thing	sick	uncomfortable	good	many
To Compare 2 Things	sicker	more uncomfortable	better	more
To Compare 3 or More Things	sickest	most uncomfortable	best	most

I am **sick** today, but I was **sicker** yesterday. Monday was the **most uncomfortable** day of all. I am **more comfortable** today.

Try It

A. Write the correct adjective to complete each sentence.

1. I have a really _____ big _____ game on Saturday.
    big / bigger

2–3. So when I came down with the _____ worst _____ sore throat in the world, I
    worse / worst
was the _____ most frightened _____ ever.
    more frightened / most frightened

4. I wanted to ignore it, but Mom thought it would be a _____ better _____
    better / best
idea to go to the doctor.

5. I was _____ afraid _____ the doctor would say I couldn't play on Saturday.
    afraid / more afraid

6. Then my _____ most horrible _____ fear would come true, and I would miss the game.
    horriblest / most horrible

B. Write the correct form of the adjective in parentheses.

7. It was the _____ longest _____ wait ever at the doctor's office. **(long)**

8. I was even _____ more nervous _____ than before I arrived. **(nervous)**

9. Then I heard the _____ scariest _____ news of all. I had strep throat. **(scary)**

10. The doctor had some _____ better _____ news than that for me, though. **(good)**

C. Complete each sentence to tell about being sick. What did you miss? Use comparative and superlative adjectives.

11. When I was sick, I felt _____.

12. That was bad, but it was even _____ when _____

_____.

13. I missed _____.

14. When I felt _____, I _____.

D. (15–18) Different things frighten different people. Write at least four sentences to tell what frightens you. Use comparative and superlative adjectives.

_____

_____

_____

_____

Edit It

E. (19–25) Edit the journal entry. Fix the seven incorrect adjectives.

September 15

Today, I had the sorest throat ever. It was
     most painful
the painfullest experience in the world to
           happy
swallow. I was happier to miss a day of

school, but I worried about missing the game.
        more
In fact, I was most worried than happy.
             best
Then, the doctor gave me the good news

ever. I had strep throat, but that wasn't the
worst
bad thing possible. I would be best for the
         better
game. What could have been best than that?

Proofreader's Marks

Change text:

healthier
I am ~~healthy~~ now than I
was before.

See all Proofreader's Marks on page ix.

71 Why Do You Need Adverbs?

To Tell *How, When,* or *Where*

- Use an **adverb** to describe a verb. Adverbs often end in **-ly**.
  - The moon shines **brightly**. (how)
  - My friend and I are camping **tonight**. (when)
  - We look **up** at the sky. (where)

- Use an **adverb** to make an adjective or another adverb stronger.
  - The woods are **extremely** quiet.
    - **adjective**
  - Our campfire burns **very** slowly.
    - **another adverb**

- Adverbs add details and bring life to your writing.
  - We are **really** content, and we talk **quietly**.
  - **Suddenly**, we hear a loud shriek.

Try It

A. **Write an adverb to make each sentence about the camping trip more interesting.**
Possible responses:

1. My friend and I ___immediately___ freeze.

2. We look all ___around___.

3. Our hearts start beating ___quickly___.

4. We feel ___very___ frightened.

5. Was the sound from a wild animal roaming ___nearby___?

B. **(6–12) Add details with adverbs.** Possible responses:

My imagination is ___extremely___ active under normal circumstances. Now it is ___really___ working overtime. I look ___up___, ___down___, and all around, but I see nothing. My friend and I get up ___quickly___ and run into the tent. Then everything gets ___eerily___ quiet. We wait ___nervously___.

157

C. What happens next? Complete the sentences to tell about a frightening experience. Use an adverb in each sentence.

13. Just then, we hear _____.

14. The loud shriek _____.

15. My friend and I _____.

16. In the end, we _____.

D. (17–20) Now use your imagination. Write at least three sentences about a place that might fill you with fear. Use at least one adverb in each sentence.

_____

_____

_____

_____

_____

Edit It

E. (21–25) Add details to the conversation. Add five adverbs. Possible responses:

Audrey: Our campfire is burning brightly, so it will keep
     animals away.

Sandra: The wind is howling, so we cannot hear what might _(fiercely)_
     be out there.

Audrey: Don't let your imagination run wild. We will wait. _(patiently)_

Sandra: Was that loud shriek an animal or a person? _(fearfully)_

Audrey: I looked and didn't see anything. It's probably the wind. _(around)_
     Let's sit. _(quietly)_

Proofreader's Marks

Add text:

frightfully
The loud noises scared
Sandra.

See all Proofreader's Marks on page ix.

158

72 What Happens When You Add *Not* to a Sentence?

You Make the Sentence Negative.

- The word **not** is an adverb. Add **not** to a sentence to make it negative. If the verb is an **action verb**, change the sentence like this:

  Jeff **enters** the house. Jeff **does** **not** **enter** the house.

- If the verb is a form of **be**, just place **not** after the verb:

  He **is** alone. He **is** **not** with anyone else.

- When you shorten a verb plus **not**, replace the **o** in **not** with an apostrophe (**'**).

  1. Jeff **does not** enter the house.   **2.** He **is not** alone.

  Jeff **doesn't** enter the house.   He **isn't** alone.

Try It

A. Rewrite each sentence. Add **not** to make it negative.

1. Jeff likes being in the big, old house. _Jeff does not (or doesn't) like being in the big, old house._

2. He feels safe. _He does not (or doesn't) feel safe._

3. The house is very quiet. _The house is not (or isn't) very quiet._

4. Jeff concentrates on reading his book. _Jeff does not (or doesn't) concentrate on reading his book._

5. The eerie noises are comforting to him. _The eerie noises are not (or aren't) comforting to him._

6. He wants to stay there overnight. _He does not (or doesn't) want to stay there overnight._

7. Jeff stops his imagination from getting the best of him. _Jeff does not (or doesn't) stop his imagination from getting the best of him._

B. Answer each question. Use not to write a negative sentence. Possible responses:

8. Is the moon shining brightly?

The moon is not (or isn't) shining brightly.

9. Are other people in the house?

Other people are not (or aren't) in the house.

10. Is the house haunted?

The house is not (or isn't) haunted.

11. Do the eerie sounds stop?

The eerie sounds do not (or don't) stop.

12. Does Jeff run out of the scary house?

Jeff does not (or doesn't) run out of the scary house.

13. Do people always imagine the worst when they are home alone?

People do not (or don't) always imagine the worst when they are home alone.

Write It

C. Complete each sentence about a house you live in or have visited. Use not to make the sentences negative.

14. The house _____.

15. I _____.

16. At night, the noises _____

_____.

D. (17–20) Write at least four negative sentences to tell about a time when your imagination ran wild and filled you with fear.

_____

_____

_____

_____

_____

73 How Do You Make a Sentence Negative?

Use One, and Only One, Negative Word.

- These words are negative words: **no, nobody, nothing, no one, not, never, nowhere,** and **none.**

- Use only one negative word in a sentence.

  Incorrect: Nobody never uses that building at night.
  Correct: Nobody ever uses that building at night.

  Incorrect: None of us could see nothing through the windows.
  Correct: None of us could see anything through the windows.

  Incorrect: We didn't have no idea who was inside.
  Correct: We didn't have any idea who was inside.
  Correct: We had no idea who was inside.

Try It

A. Fix each sentence to use only one negative word. There is more than one correct answer. Possible responses:

1. Not ~~none~~ any of the neighbors liked having the abandoned house on the street.

2. Nobody wanted ~~nothing~~ anything to do with it.

3. At least nothing suspicious ~~never~~ ever happened there.

4. Well, ~~not~~ nothing happened until last night, anyway.

5. The neighbors didn't see ~~no one~~ anyone going inside.

6. The house was not empty ~~no~~ any longer, though.

7. My friends and I couldn't imagine ~~nobody~~ anybody would want to live there.

8. Whoever was inside was ~~not~~ up to no good.

Proofreader's Marks

Delete:

I had ~~not~~ never been inside the house.

Change text:
any
Not ~~none~~ of my friends had been inside, either.

See all Proofreader's Marks on page ix.

B. Rewrite each sentence to make it a negative sentence. Possible responses:

9. Everyone wanted to go inside the house.
   No one wanted to go inside the house.

10. Then the police came and said all of us should go in.
    Then the police came and said none of us should go in.

11. So we all waited near the house.
    So we all waited nowhere near the house.

12. When the police came out, one of them was serious.
    When the police came out, not one of them was serious.

13. They did find a criminal, but they did capture a raccoon!
    They did not find a criminal, but they did capture a raccoon!

Write It

C. Imagine you found an abandoned house. Complete each sentence to tell about your experience. Use a negative word in each sentence.

14. The old, abandoned house _____

    _____.

15. I thought _____

    _____.

16. At first, my imagination went wild, but then I found out _____

    _____.

D. (17–20) Write a police report. Write at least four sentences about what you found in the abandoned house. Use at least four negative words.

_____

_____

_____

_____

_____

74 Can You Use an Adverb to Make a Comparison?

Yes, But You Need to Change the Adverb.

- Adverbs have different forms. Use the form that fits your purpose.

To Describe 1 Action	fast	fitfully	well	badly
To Compare 2 Actions	faster	more fitfully	better	worse
To Compare 3 or More Actions	fastest	most fitfully	best	worst

- How many things are being compared in these sentences?

   Last week, I slept the **most fitfully** that I've ever slept on a camping trip.

   I'll enjoy this camping trip **better** than I enjoyed the last camping trip.

Try It

A. Write the correct adverb to describe the action in each sentence.

1. We heard something shriek _____ more fiercely _____ than usual.

more fiercely / most fiercely

2. My imagination worked the _____ most furiously _____ ever.

more furiously / most furiously

3. Things turned out _____ more unexpectedly _____ than I imagined.

more unexpectedly / most unexpectedly

4. We laughed _____ loudly _____ when we discovered a lost cat.

loudly / more loudly

5. This week's trip started _____ better _____ than last week's.

better / best

B. Write the correct form of the adverb in parentheses to complete each sentence.

6. Then it started to rain _____ more fiercely _____ than I've ever seen. **(fiercely)**

7. It rained the _____ hardest _____ of all at night. **(hard)**

8. We heard thunder roaring _____ loudly _____ through the woods. **(loudly)**

9. We saw lightning flashing the _____ most brightly _____ ever. **(brightly)**

10. I waited _____ more desperately _____ than before for the storm to end. **(desperately)**

Write It

C. Describe a rainstorm that would make your imagination work overtime. Use adverbs that compare.

11. The wind blows _____.

12. The rain falls _____.

13. Thunder roars _____.

14. Lightning flashes _____.

D. (15–19) Now imagine that you are in a tent in the woods at night. Write at least five sentences to tell what would make your imagination work overtime. Use adverbs that compare.

_____

_____

_____

_____

_____

Edit It

E. (20–25) Edit the journal entry. Fix the six incorrect adverbs.

June 10

I think my camping days are over! Last
week, I waited anxiously for morning because
an animal was shrieking ~~most~~ (more) loudly than I
had heard before. Last night, I waited even (more)
anxiously for the rainstorm to end. Then the
wind was blowing the ~~more~~ (most) furiously ever. The
thunder roared the ~~more~~ (most) deafeningly ever. The
lightning scared me the ~~worse~~ (worst) of all. I think I'll
sleep (more) happily in my own bed than in a tent!

Proofreader's Marks

Change text:
It rained ~~hard~~ (harder) this week than last week.

Delete:
It rained ~~more~~ harder this week than last week.

Add text:
It rained (harder) this week than last week.

See all Proofreader's Marks on page ix.

164

75 Use Adverbs Correctly

Remember: You can use adverbs to describe and compare actions.
An adverb can also make another adverb or an adjective stronger.

Describe	Compare	Make Stronger
I went **hesitantly** to the scary movie.	The music blared **more frightfully** than before.	It was a **really** scary movie.
I watched **fearfully**.	I screamed the **most loudly** ever.	I was **very** scared.

Try It

A. Write adverbs to add details to the sentences. Possible responses:

1. I _____usually_____ like scary movies.

2. This movie was _____exceptionally_____ scary, though.

3. The music blared the most _____frightfully_____ ever.

4. The special effects were _____especially_____ scary.

5. Once, I jumped _____suddenly_____ in my seat.

B. Complete each sentence. Write the correct form of the adverb in parentheses.

6. This movie was made from the _____most amazingly_____ scary book of all time. **(amazingly)**

7. The movie scared me even _____worse_____ than the book did. **(badly)**

8. It seemed to be _____more thoroughly_____ suspenseful than the book. **(thoroughly)**

9. I was so _____incredibly_____ scared that I had to close my eyes. **(incredibly)**

10. Don't see this movie unless you want to see the _____most intensely_____ scary movie in the world! **(intensely)**

Write It

C. Answer the questions to tell about a scary movie you have seen. Use the correct forms of adverbs in your answers.

11. What was the most incredibly scary movie you have ever seen? _____

_____

12. Why was the movie so very scary? _____

_____

13. Which scene was the most thoroughly scary of all? What did you do when you watched

that scene? _____

_____

_____

D. (14–16) Write at least three sentences about a scary movie that triggered your imagination. Use adverbs to describe what you did and how you felt after the movie.

_____

_____

_____

_____

_____

Edit It

E. (17–20) Edit the paragraph. Fix the four incorrect adverbs.

I have the most incredibly active imagination in the world. When I am home alone, all the normally innocent-sounding house noises resonate more suspiciously like intruders. If I'm camping, every sound is a wild animal snarling most ferociously than the one before. When I'm writing a story, though, my imagination works most best. I write better rapidly when I am scared. I imagine many good ideas to write creatively about!

Proofreader's Marks

Change text:
I listen ~~most~~ more carefully when I'm home alone than when my family is home.

Delete:
I listen ~~more~~ better when I'm home alone than when my family is home.

See all Proofreader's Marks on page ix.

166

✓ Capitalize Quotations Correctly

- Capitalize the first word of a direct quotation that is a complete sentence.

    "**How** much is the book?" asked Anil.

    The bookstore clerk replied, "**It's** $9.95, but it might be on sale."

- Do not capitalize the first word of the second part of a direct quotation when it is a continuation of the sentence.

    "I'd like to buy it," said Anil, "**if** it's on sale."

    "In that case," said the clerk, "**let** me find out for sure if it's on sale."

Try It

A. Use proofreader's marks to correct the capitalization error in each sentence.

1. "this is my favorite book," Darius said.

2. Kim asked, "why is it your favorite book?"

3. "I like it," he replied, "Because the story is suspenseful and exciting."

Proofreader's Marks

Capitalize:

The man said, "i hope you like the book." ≡

Do not capitalize:

"Yes," I said, "M̶e, too."

See all Proofreader's Marks on page ix.

B. Rewrite the following sentences as direct quotations. Be sure to use the correct capitalization. The first one is done for you.

4. He told me I should read this book because he thought I would really like it. ___"You should read this book," he said, "because I think you will really like it."___

5. I asked him who the author of the book was. ___"Who is the author of the book?" I asked.___

6. He replied that Luke Samuelson was the author. ___He replied, "Luke Samuelson is the author."___

7. I said excitedly that he was one of my favorite authors. ___"He is one of my favorite authors!" I said excitedly.___

✔ Use Quotation Marks Correctly

- Use **quotation marks** when writing the exact words that a person said.
  Samantha said, "I'm going to the bookstore."
  "Why?" asked Andrew. "What do you need there?"

- Do not use quotation marks when describing what a person said.
  Samantha said that she needed a new book to read.

- Use a comma to set off tags, or words that identify who is quoted.
  "I'm going to go with you to the bookstore," said Andrew.
  "Hurry up," said Samantha, "because I'm leaving right now."

Try It

A. (8–17) Add or remove quotation marks and commas where necessary. Use proofreader's marks.

> Jesse was waiting in line at the local bookstore to meet Angela Rivera, his favorite author.
>
> "I hope I can get her autograph," he muttered.
>
> Just then, the manager said "there was only time for five more autographs." Jesse was the twelfth person in line. "I'll at least get a close look at her," he thought with disappointment."
>
> "Young man," said a pleasant voice, "why do you look so sad?"
>
> Jesse looked up and saw Angela Rivera standing in front of him. "You're my favorite author, he replied, "and I really wanted to meet you, but I was too far back in line."
>
> "I always have time for my fans," she said. "Give me your books, and I'll sign them for you."
>
> As he left the bookstore, Jesse thought he was the luckiest person in the world.

Proofreader's Marks

Add quotation marks:
"Can I have the book?"
she asked.

Add a comma:
"Of course you can" he
said.

Delete:
He hoped ~~she was~~
happy with the book.

✓Use Correct Paragraph Structure

A **paragraph** is a group of sentences that tell about the same idea. Organize sentences about the same idea into one paragraph. The **topic sentence** tells about the main, or controlling, idea of the paragraph.

Incorrect	Correct
Jan tried to put the book on the shelf, but it fell back into her bag.	**Jan tried to put the book on the shelf, but it fell back into her bag.** Then she spied the gray lady
Then she spied the gray lady watching her.	watching her. Jan's thoughts raced. What should she do or say?
Jan's thoughts raced. What should she do or say?	**Carefully, Jan reached into her bag and removed the book.** All the while
Carefully, Jan reached into her bag and removed the book. All the while the gray lady was watching.	the gray lady was watching.

Try It

A. (18–20) Rewrite the story. Organize the sentences so that they follow the correct paragraph structure. You will have to make three changes.

Cara loved to write short stories, but she was too scared to share them with anyone.

She was afraid that people would make fun of her. Then one day, Mr. Marquez gave the class an assignment to write a short story and then read it aloud to the class. Cara felt a clench in her stomach. How would she be able to stand up in front of the class and read her story?

She would have to tell Mr. Marquez that she couldn't do the assignment.

Cara loved to write short stories, but she was too scared to share them with anyone. She was afraid that people would make fun of her.

Then one day, Mr. Marquez gave the class an assignment to write a short story and then read it aloud to the class. Cara felt a clench in her stomach. How would she be able to stand up in front of the class and read her story? She would have to tell Mr. Marquez that she couldn't do the assignment.

✓Use Adjectives and Adverbs Correctly

- Use a **comparative adjective** to show how two things are alike or different. Add **-er** to a short adjective to make it comparative. Use **more** or **less** with a long adjective.

    The book I read was short, but your book was even **shorter**.

    Which book was **more interesting**?

- Use an **adverb** to describe a verb or make an adjective or another adverb stronger. Do not use an adjective instead of an adverb. Remember that adverbs often end in **-ly**.

    My book is **really** long.
           adverb adjective

    I **quickly** read it last night.
     adverb   verb

    In fact, I read it **very** quickly.
              another adverb

Try It

A. Choose the correct form of the adjective or adverb in each sentence.

21. The _____*amazingly*_____ talented young writer just published her second novel.
         amazing / amazingly

22. Critics gave her first novel rave reviews, but they think this one is even
_____*more wonderful*_____.
wonderfuller / more wonderful

23. The book is _____*rapidly*_____ selling out in bookstores everywhere.
      rapid / rapidly

24. The young writer is _____*extremely*_____ grateful for her success.
      extreme / extremely

25. She doesn't think she could be any _____*luckier*_____ than she already is.
      luckier / more lucky

76 What's a Simple Sentence?

A Sentence with One Subject and One Predicate

You can express a complete thought with a simple sentence. In statements, the subject usually comes before the predicate.

Subject	Predicate
Our **class** noun	**studied** advertising last week. verb
Certain food **advertisements** noun	**target** teenagers. verb
The **teacher** noun	**conducted** a taste test in class. verb
The **students** noun	**tasted** three snacks and chose the best. verb

Try It

A. Identify the following phrases as a subject or predicate. Then write a complete sentence by adding the missing part. Possible responses:

1. Our class __subject; Our class had a taste test.__

2. tasted snacks. __predicate; Each student tasted snacks.__

3. The snacks __subject; The snacks were familiar to us.__

4. chose my favorite snack. __predicate; I chose my favorite snack.__

B. Add a predicate to each subject. Then underline the noun in the subject once and the verb in the predicate twice. Possible responses:

5. Many <u>advertisements</u> __are false.__

6. <u>People</u> everywhere __see advertisements.__

7. The <u>students</u> __in my class discuss advertisements.__

C. Answer the questions about an advertisement you like. Use simple sentences.

   8. Which advertisements do you like? I like _____.

   9. What is memorable or special about the advertisement? _____ is memorable

   because _____.

   10. What does the advertisement claim about the product? _____

   _____

   11. What emotions does the advertisement bring out in you? _____

   _____

D. (12–15) Write at least four simple sentences about advertisements you have seen recently.

   _____

   _____

   _____

   _____

   _____

   _____

Edit It

E. (16–20) Edit the advertisement. Fix the five mistakes in subjects and predicates.
Possible responses:

Hearty Oatmeal Cookies

Teens need healthy snacks. ~~love~~ Teens love Hearty Oatmeal Cookies.
Hearty Oatmeal Cookies are the healthiest cookies around. They
have an all-natural taste just like homemade cookies. They have no sugar.
Everyone loves Hearty Oatmeal Cookies.

Proofreader's Marks
Add text: are Some ads entertaining.
See all Proofreader's Marks on page ix.

172

77 Does the Subject Always Come First?

Not Always

In questions, the **verb** often comes before the subject.

- **Was** the taste **test** surprising?

  verb   subject

  verb . . . . verb
- **Can you predict** the most popular snack?

       subject

In some statements, the verb comes before the subject.

- Here **are** the **results** of the taste test.

      verb   subject
- **Is** this **result** ever unexpected!

  verb   subject

Try It

A. Complete each sentence about the taste test. Use the correct verb form.

1. _____**Do**_____ you think that people buy snacks because of the packaging?
   Do / Does

2. How _____**does**_____ the class rate the unfamiliar brands?
   does / do

3. Here _____**is**_____ the highest-rated snack. It is not a well-known brand.
   is / are

4. _____**Was**_____ this result ever a surprise!
   Was / Were

B. Put the words in the right order and write the question. Place the verb before the subject.

5. brands? / you / buy / Do / unknown _Do you buy unknown brands?_

6. less / Are / expensive? / they _Are they less expensive?_

7. they / taste / Do / good? _Do they taste good?_

C. Answer the questions about advertising and packaging methods. Place the verb
before the subject in some of your sentences.

8. What unknown brand foods have you tried and liked? _____

9. How did advertising influence your knowledge about the products? _____

_____

10. How do these products affect your opinion of unknown brands? _____

_____

11. What factors determine the products that people choose? For example, are commercials,

packaging, or friends' recommendations important? _____

_____

D. (12–15) Write at least four sentences about the advertising or packaging of
a product. In one sentence, place the verb before the subject.

_____

_____

_____

_____

_____

Edit It

E. (16–20) Edit the paragraph. For each sentence, reverse the order of
subject and verb. Edits will include adding words, deleting words,
changing punctuation, and capitalizing words.

Are unknown brands *are* sometimes better than well-known brands?
Do people tend to choose the most interesting wrapper or
package? Do packaging and advertising influence our choices?
Are commercials and advertisements *are* not helpful. Never did a single
never did commercial or wrapper tell me how a product tastes.

Proofreader's Marks
Delete:
Does this ad ~~makes~~ make the snack tastier?
Add text:
This brand is *not* well-known.
Capitalize:
advertising affects us.
Add period:
I enjoy many snacks⊙
See all Proofreader's Marks on page ix.

78 What's an Infinitive?

To + a Verb

Use **to** plus a **verb** to form an **infinitive**. An infinitive acts like a noun, an adverb, or an adjective.

- Like all nouns, an infinitive can be the **object** of an **action verb**.

  We **need to sell** more tickets. Who **wants to suggest** a strategy?

verb infinitive   verb   infinitive

- You can also use an infinitive in the **subject** of a sentence. The **verb** will always be singular.

  To sell tickets to the concert **is** our main goal.

infinitive   verb

- You can also use an infinitive as an adjective or an adverb.

  Advertising **is** a way **to sell** tickets. Let's **have** a meeting **to share** ideas.

verb   infinitive as   verb   infinitive as

            an adjective   an adverb

Try It

A. **(1–4) Complete each sentence with an infinitive.**   Possible responses:

Hemin wanted _____*to post*_____ flyers around our neighborhoods.
____*To advertise*____ our concert on the radio was Maria's idea. Another student
hoped _____*to place*_____ an ad in the community newspaper. We each try
_____*to sell*_____ some tickets every day, and so far we're doing great!

B. Complete each sentence using an infinitive from the box. Write **subject**, **object**, **adjective**, or **adverb** to tell how the infinitive was used.

> to advertise   to mail   to reach

5. Our gymnastics team wants _____*to advertise*_____ our competitions to boost attendance.
____*object*____

6. We will use the student directory _____*to reach*_____ all students. ____*adverb*____

7. ____*To mail*____ our announcements is expensive but worth it. ____*subject*____

175

Write It

C. Answer the questions about advertising for a school-related event. Use infinitives as an object, a subject, an adjective, or an adverb.

8. How did you help to advertise an event? I helped _____.

9. To advertise effectively, what steps did you take? _____
   _____

10. Who worked with you to carry out your plan? _____

11. Will you try to advertise another event in the future? Why or why not? _____
   _____

D. (12–16) Write at least five sentences about effective advertising. Use infinitives in your sentences.

_____
_____
_____
_____
_____

Edit It

E. (17–20) Edit the advertisement. Fix the four mistakes in infinitives.

School Musical

Please come and show your support for our theater club. To
put on a musical ~~require~~ requires hard work and dedication. To perform
before a full house ~~are~~ is what our talented cast deserves. The show
will take place in the high school auditorium. We hope to see you
there on April 22 at 8:00 p.m. We don't want you to miss the best
production of the year!

Proofreader's Marks

Change text:
To act ~~are~~ is a challenge.

Add text:
                    to
They hope sell 300 tickets.

See all Proofreader's Marks on page ix.

176

79 Can a Verb Act Like a Noun?

Yes, When It Is a Gerund.

Add **-ing** to a **verb** to form a **gerund**. A gerund acts like a noun in a sentence.

- A gerund is often the **object** of an **action verb**.

  We **like raising** money for our school. James **loves counting** the
     verb   gerund   verb   gerund
  tickets we sell.

- You can also use a gerund as the **object** of a **preposition**.
  Summertime is a tough time **for fundraising**.
                                             gerund

- Like all nouns, a gerund is often the **subject** of a sentence.
  The **verb** will always be singular.
  Selling for fundraisers **involves** many challenges.
   gerund   verb

  Having confidence **is** important for success.
   gerund   verb

Try It

A. Complete each sentence about fundraising. Choose a verb from the box. Change it to a gerund by adding -ing.

ask	eat	get	hold	raise	sell

1. The fall is a good time for _____ holding _____ a school fundraiser.

2. _____ Raising _____ funds through candy sales is usually very effective.

3. For many students, _____ asking _____ people to buy the candy is difficult.

4. Sheila dislikes _____ selling _____ things because she is shy.

5. Pedro dislikes _____ eating _____ candy, so he has difficulty claiming that people will enjoy it.

6. _____ Getting _____ people to support a fundraiser is hard work!

B. Complete each sentence by changing the verb in parentheses to a gerund. Then write how it is used in the sentence, as a **subject** or an **object**, at the end of the sentence.

7. ___Buying___ a raffle ticket shows support of our school. **(buy)** ___subject___

8. It is difficult to sell raffle tickets without ___advertising___. **(advertise)** ___object___

9. People like ___buying___ raffle tickets when they know it is for a good cause. **(buy)** ___object___

10. Still, ___convincing___ people to buy a raffle ticket can be difficult. **(convince)** ___subject___

11. I like ___selling___ tickets, and I tend to raise a lot of money. **(sell)** ___object___

12. I enjoy ___raising___ more money than anyone else in our class! **(raise)** ___object___

Write It

C. Answer the questions about participating in a fundraiser. Use gerunds in your sentences.

13. Tell about a time you helped with fundraising. _____

14. What were some of the challenges of selling? _____

15. How did advertising affect your sales? _____

16. Was explaining the fundraiser easy or difficult for you? Why? _____

17. What did your experience teach you about fundraising? _____

_____

D. (18–20) Write at least three suggestions for students who plan to participate in a fundraiser. Use a gerund in each sentence.

_____

_____

_____

_____

_____

80 Vary Your Sentences

Remember: Your sentences are more interesting when you vary the word order and the types of sentences you write.

To vary your sentences, you can:

- Place a **verb** before the **subject**.
  First **comes price**. Then there **are** other **priorities** when I shop.

- Expand a sentence with an **infinitive phrase**.
  Popular labels influence some teenagers.
  Popular labels influence some teenagers **to buy products**.
  _____ infinitive phrase

- Use a **gerund** or an **infinitive** as the subject of your sentence.
  Remember that these subjects always take a **singular verb**.
  To buy something just for the label **is** often expensive. **Considering**
  infinitive   gerund
  both the label and the price **shows** wisdom.

Try It

A. Rewrite each sentence. Change the underlined part to a gerund or infinitive.

1. <u>To buy clothes</u> is fun for my friend and me. _Buying clothes is fun for my friend and me._

2. <u>Getting</u> a good deal is always my priority. _To get a good deal is always my priority._

3. I do not like <u>to spend</u> all of my money on popular labels. _I do not like spending all of my money on popular labels._

4. My friend likes <u>spending</u> lots of money for popular labels. _My friend likes to spend lots of money for popular labels._

5. <u>Saying</u> who looks more stylish is difficult. _To say who looks more stylish is difficult._

B. (6–11) Complete each sentence with an infinitive or gerund using verbs from the box. Possible responses:

buy	find	get	learn	purchase	spend

_____Buying_____ products is fun for my friends and me. ___To purchase___ high-quality products is important. _____Spending_____ too much money is not an option for me. My goal is always _____to find_____ a good sale. I try ___to research___ the products ahead of time to learn the prices. I love _____getting_____ any product at a great price.

Write It

C. Answer the questions about shopping. Vary your sentences by including infinitives, gerunds, or verb-subject word order.

12. Do you enjoy shopping? I _____.

13. What are your priorities when buying clothes and other products? My priorities are

_____.

14. What can you do to learn about products? _____

_____

15. How do advertisements affect your decisions when buying products? _____

_____

16. Does advertising help you make a decision? If so, how? _____

_____

D. (17–20) Write at least four sentences that describe methods advertisers use to sell products. Use gerunds and infinitives.

_____

_____

_____

_____

_____

81 How Are Phrases and Clauses Different?

A Clause Has a Subject and a Predicate.

- A **phrase** is a group of words that function together. One sentence often has several phrases.

  My favorite television **series** / **shows** / a family / with teenage children.

      noun phrase   verb   noun phrase   adjective phrase

  This sentence is complete because it has a **subject** and a **verb**.
  A phrase never has both, so it does not express a complete thought.

- A **clause** contains a **subject** and a **verb**. It can stand alone as a sentence.

  The last **episode** **was** funny.

  My **friends** **watch** this show, too.

Try It

A. On the line, write one phrase from each sentence. Possible responses:

1. My favorite show airs on Thursday evenings. __on Thursday evenings__

2. The main characters seem like ordinary teenagers. __The main characters__

3. The parents help the teens with problems. __with problems__

4. Their solutions work more smoothly than those in real life. __Their solutions__

B. Include each phrase in a sentence about a TV game show. Possible responses:

5. every afternoon __John likes a show that airs every afternoon.__

6. the game show host __The game show host has a good sense of humor.__

7. the main contestant can win __The main contestant can win several thousand dollars.__

8. the other contestants __The other contestants receive rewards also.__

C. Answer the questions about television shows you watch. Be sure to use phrases and clauses correctly.

9. What television shows do you and your friends watch? My friends and I _____

_____ .

10. Which are your favorite shows, and why? My favorite shows _____ .

11. Who are your favorite characters in the shows? _____

12. How are the characters similar to and different from you? _____

_____

D. (13–16) Write at least four more sentences about television shows you like. Be sure to use phrases and clauses correctly.

_____

_____

_____

_____

Edit It

E. (17–20) Edit the newspaper editorial. Fix the four mistakes to make the sentences complete.

> I support minority television channels. Growing up, I watched. Shows about families who are different from my own family. I never felt the connection my schoolmates did. When they talked about those shows. Then I watched. A minority channel. Felt instantly connected to the shows that mirror my life and culture.

Proofreader's Marks
Add text: many Sarai likes television shows. ∧
Delete: The main character has interesting problems.
Do not capitalize: Television Shows vary widely.
See all Proofreader's Marks on page ix.

182

82 What's a Compound Sentence?
Two Clauses Joined by *And*, *But*, or *Or*

The words **and**, **but**, and **or** are conjunctions. They join the two clauses
in a **compound sentence**. A comma (**,**) comes before the conjunction.

- Use **and** to join similar ideas.

  People watch celebrities on television.
  Celebrities influence viewers in many ways.

  People watch celebrities on television, and celebrities influence viewers in many ways.

- Use **but** to join different ideas.

  Some celebrities support great causes.
  People often do not learn about them.

  Some celebrities support great causes, but people often do not learn about them.

- Use **or** to show a choice.

  Fans dress like their favorite musicians.
  Fans can develop their own style.

  Fans dress like their favorite musicians, or they can develop their own style.

Try It

A. Combine each pair of sentences. Use and, but, or or to make a compound sentence.

1. Celebrities influence society. Some of them are excellent
   role models.
   , and (inserted)

2. Some teenagers wear clothes like those of their favorite
   musicians. Others try to look different from everyone else.
   , but (inserted)

3. People imitate the risky behaviors of some celebrities.
   People follow the example of celebrities who work hard.
   , or (inserted)

4. Some teenagers want to look glamorous and stylish like
   celebrities. Others accept themselves the way they are.
   , but (inserted)

5. People can buy products that celebrities advertise. They can buy products based on
   personal research.
   , or (inserted)

Proofreader's Marks

Delete:
    You can wear ~~/~~ anything you
    want.

Add a comma and text:
    I watch movies on TV I also
    watch the news. *, and*

Do not capitalize:
    Television ~~S~~hows can be
    interesting.

See all Proofreader's Marks
on page ix.

B. Choose the correct conjunction to combine the two related sentences.

6. Celebrities get a lot of attention, _____ and _____ they often use it wisely.
and / or

7. Some celebrities are good role models, _____ but _____ others set a bad example.
or / but

8. My favorite celebrity supports environmental causes, _____ and _____ she
and / but
appears in an advertisement to save the rainforest.

9. Some celebrities say that they support certain causes, _____ but _____ their
or / but
actions don't reflect what they say.

10. You can choose to listen to what a celebrity says, _____ or _____ you can
and / or
make decisions based on your own research.

Write It

C. Answer the questions below. Use compound sentences in your responses.

11. Which television shows and magazines discuss the lives of celebrities? Which do you
like or dislike? _____, and _____.

12. Is the information in these sources reliable? _____

13. When you hear or read about a celebrity, how can you tell if the information is true?

_____

14. How does the information affect people's opinions about celebrities? _____

_____

15. Is it fair for television and magazines to write about celebrities' families, childhoods, or
relationships? _____

D. (16–20) Write at least four compound sentences about how celebrities are
portrayed in the media and whether you think these portrayals are accurate.

_____

_____

_____

_____

83 What's a Run-on Sentence?

A Sentence That Goes On and On

- To fix a run-on sentence, break it into shorter sentences.

  Run On: There are many television shows to choose from **and** I like entertainment shows **but** sometimes I also watch the news.

  Better: There are many television shows to choose from. I like entertainment shows, but sometimes I also watch the news.

- Sometimes you can also rearrange words to express the same idea.

  Run On: Local news is one kind of news show **and** national news is a different type of news show **and** so is international news.

  Better: Local, national, and international are different types of news shows.

Try It

A. Edit the three sentences that are run-ons. Possible responses:

1. Paula likes to watch celebrity news and I see why it interests her but I prefer to watch the national and international news.

2. I want to know about events that affect my life, and I feel news about celebrities does not impact me closely. not a run-on

3. I question whether celebrity news is true and the national news seems biased sometimes but I can watch reports on different channels to check.

4. Sometimes Paula visits me and she wants to watch her favorite celebrity news channels but I watch the news as always and she usually becomes interested, too.

Proofreader's Marks
Add a period: People are interested in celebrities⊙
Add a comma: This news is shocking⌃ but is it true?
Delete: He likes this show, and and I see why.
See all Proofreader's Marks on page ix.

B. Revise each run-on sentence to make two or more shorter sentences. Possible responses:

5. Everyone I know prefers a different news channel and my teacher likes the international news but my parents like local news. _Everyone I know prefers a different news channel. My teacher likes the international news, but my parents like local news._

6. My grandfather says that all news is biased but my father says that some channels are more biased than others and he reads the newspaper to double-check the perspective of others. _My grandfather says that all news is biased, but my father says that some channels are more biased than others. He reads the newspaper to double-check the perspective of others._

7. My teacher prefers to watch the national news and she believes it is important to keep up with politics and changes in laws and she insists that these changes always affect us. _My teacher prefers to watch the national news. She believes it is important to keep up with politics and changes in laws. She insists that these changes always affect us._

Write It

C. Express your opinions about popular television programming by answering the following questions. Check that your answers do not include run-on sentences.

8. What types of television shows do you prefer? _I prefer television shows _____ _____._

9. Why do different people like to watch different types of shows? _____ _____

10. Are television shows better for learning or for entertainment? _____

D. (11–15) Write at least five additional sentences about your opinions on television programming. Make sure not to use run-on sentences.

_____

_____

_____

_____

_____

84 How Do You Fix a Run-on Sentence?

Break It into Shorter Sentences.

- Some run-on sentences include too many phrases or clauses divided by **commas**.

  Everyone in my family has different interests, and this affects the television shows they like to watch, and this makes perfect sense, I love cooking, so I watch a cooking show almost every day.

- To fix, create shorter, more understandable sentences.

  Everyone in my family has different interests. This affects the television shows we like to watch. This makes perfect sense. I love cooking, so I watch a cooking show almost every day.

Try It

A. Fix each run-on sentence by creating shorter sentences. Punctuate each sentence correctly.

1. My family watches television after dinner and we like to watch shows together but it is difficult to agree on one channel, though.

2. My brother insists on watching game shows but I don't like game shows and my parents always want to see the news.

3. My sister reads the newspaper and news on the Internet and she doesn't want to review news again and she prefers to see reruns of her favorite comedy.

4. We all like reruns of my sister's favorite sit-com and we often watch them and we also make sure to watch a game show from time to time for my brother.

5. Sometimes I feel that we should watch the news out of respect for our parents but they watch the news anyway and they just watch it after we go to bed.

Proofreader's Marks

Delete:

The news can be informative, ~~but~~ and it can be interesting.

Capitalize:

television shows vary widely.

Add a period:

Some sit-coms are funnier than others⊙

See all Proofreader's Marks on page ix.

B. Revise these run-on sentences by forming short, understandable sentences about families and their hobbies.

6. My family members all have different interests, and my father loves to go fishing, my mother enjoys gardening, and my sister and I like listening to music. _My family members all have different interests. My father loves to go fishing. My mother enjoys gardening. My sister and I like listening to music._

7. One thing we do together is watch television, also we have a great system of deciding what shows to watch, and we certainly need it. _One thing we do together is watch television. We have a great system of deciding what shows to watch. We certainly need it._

8. We watch a different show every evening, and everyone gets to choose the show at least one night every week, and if other family members don't want to watch it, they don't have to. _We watch a different show every evening. Everyone gets to choose the show at least one night every week. If other family members don't want to watch it, they don't have to._

Write It

C. Write about your favorite forms of entertainment. Fix any run-on sentences.

9. What types of hobbies do you enjoy? I enjoy _____.

10. How does the time you spend on hobbies compare to the amount of time you watch television? I spend more time _____.

11. What time of the day do you find yourself working on different hobbies? _____

_____

D. (12–15) Write at least four sentences that tell more about your interests and hobbies. Be sure to avoid run-on sentences.

_____

_____

_____

_____

_____

(85) Use Compound Sentences

Remember: A compound sentence includes two independent clauses joined by **and**, **but**, or **or**.

- Use **and** to join like ideas. Use **but** to join different ideas. Use **or** to show a choice.

  My friends and I know that television is not often realistic, **and** we want to learn about the real world. We want to visit different cultures, cities, and countries, **but** we are limited. We need to earn a lot of extra money, **or** we need to convince our parents to pay our way.

- Don't overuse **and**.

  To learn about the world, we watch video documentaries about different countries and cities ~~and~~ ⊙ We visiting museum exhibits on world cultures ⊙ Also, we ~~and~~ watching foreign films.

Try It

A. Edit the sentences. Form compound sentences by using **and, but,** and **or** when appropriate. Avoid overusing the conjunction **and**.

Possible responses:

1. I ride the bus with my mother ⊙ ~~and~~ we visit many parts of town , and I learn about my city.

2. My brother and I read the city paper to learn about our community ⊙ ~~and~~ we like to look for jobs that we might want and we read about new programs for teenagers.

3. The newspaper tells about the city ⊙ ~~and~~ many of my friends want to experience it but they cannot travel ⊙ They ~~and~~ use the Internet to research pictures , or They read articles about different countries.

4. Television shows showcase different cities and cultures ⊙ ~~and~~ sometimes they are realistic but documentaries tell more about the real world than most dramas or comedies.

Proofreader's Marks

Add a period:

I like the travel channel ⊙

Add a comma:

They ask the teacher and they visit the media center.

Delete:

Trains are fun, ~~and~~ but planes are fast.

Capitalize:

i like to see new places.
=

Add text:
                    and
Check out books, read magazines, visit Web sites.

See all Proofreader's Marks on page ix.

189

B. Form correct compound sentences about ways television affects our view of the world. Use **and**, **but**, and **or** when appropriate. Avoid overusing the conjunction **and**.

5. Television makes the world look brighter than it is. The real world is not as beautiful as the one on TV. _Television makes the world look brighter than it is, but the real world is not as beautiful as the one on TV._

6. Houses in shows are perfectly clean. Outside settings look unnaturally beautiful. _Houses in shows are perfectly clean, and outside settings look unnaturally beautiful._

7. Television sometimes shows the world as simple. Problems in the real world are not that simple. _Television sometimes shows the world as simple, but problems in the real world are not that simple._

8. My friends want to know about real life in other countries. They want to learn about other cultures. _My friends want to know about real life in other countries, and they want to learn about other cultures._

Write It

C. Answer the questions about differences you have noticed between real life and television. Use compound sentences correctly in your answers.

9. How do people on television look and act differently from people in real life? People on TV _____.

10. How do images on television affect people's feelings about real life? _____

_____.

11. How do images on television relate to real life? _____

_____.

D. (12–15) Write at least four more compound sentences about ways that television relates to real life. Avoid overusing the conjunction **and**.

_____

_____

_____

_____

86 What's a Complex Sentence?

A Sentence with Two Kinds of Clauses

- A clause has a **subject** and a **verb**. An **independent clause** can stand alone as a sentence.

  <u>**I** **saw** a protest.</u>
  independent clause

- A **dependent clause** also has a subject and a verb. But it cannot stand alone because it begins with a **conjunction**.

  <u>when my **family** **went** downtown</u>
  dependent clause

- You can use the conjunction to "hook" the dependent clause to an independent clause. The new sentence is complete, and it is called a **complex sentence**.

  <u>**I** **saw** a protest</u> <u>when my **family** **went** downtown.</u>
  independent clause   dependent clause

Try It

A. Form complex sentences about news coverage. Draw a line to connect each independent clause with a dependent clause.

1. We saw about one hundred protesters   because it claimed that there were "several" marchers who "behaved badly."

2. We parked close to the protest   when we were driving.

3. The people remained calm and orderly   as they marched silently to protest their wages.

4. The next morning we read about the march in the newspaper   because we wanted to read the signs.

5. We were surprised by the article   as we ate breakfast.

6. The article exaggerated   because most people were well behaved.

B. Write whether each clause is independent or dependent. If dependent, rewrite it to create a complex sentence. If independent, punctuate it correctly to form a sentence. Possible responses:

7. the media can shape people's impressions ___ independent; The media can shape people's impressions.

8. when an incident took place recently at the football game ___ dependent; I was there to witness it when an incident took place recently at the football game.

9. but a few fans argued ___ dependent; Most people were well behaved, but a few fans argued.

10. a reporter wrote about it ___ independent; A reporter wrote about it.

Write It

C. Answer the questions about media coverage of events. Use complex sentences.

11. What incident do you know about that the media reported with bias? I know that

_____.

12. How do you think the reports affected people's perceptions? _____

13. What did this event and its coverage teach you about the media? _____

14. If events are reported with bias, how can you learn the truth about what you read?

_____

15. When you detect bias in a source, do you continue to read it? Why or why not?

_____

D. (16–20) Write at least five sentences about bias in media reporting. Include complex sentences in your responses.

_____

_____

_____

_____

_____

87 Can a Clause Act Like an Adverb?

Yes, and It Often Tells When or Why.

- A **complex sentence** has one independent clause and one dependent clause.

  Newspapers include photographs <u>because they help readers understand events.</u>

  independent clause   dependent clause

- When the **dependent clause** acts like an adverb, it begins with a **subordinating conjunction**. The conjunction shows how the two clauses are related.

Tells When:	**After** I came home from school, I flipped through a magazine.
Tells Why:	**Since** I took exams all day, I now want to read for enjoyment.
Tells What May Happen:	I will read any article **if it has an interesting photo**.

- More **conjunctions** include: before, when, whenever, while, until, because, unless, although.

Try It

A. Create complex sentences about photographs that illustrate news articles. Add a clause that begins with a subordinating conjunction. Possible responses:

1. I read the article about the game _because it included an interesting_ _photograph._

2. ___Although the article described the game in depth___, the photograph conveyed additional details, such as the emotions of the players.

3. I let my friend borrow the newspaper ___when I finished reading the article___.

4. ___After my friend read the article___, we talked about parts of the game.

5. We didn't remember how exciting it was ___until we saw the photograph___.

B. Complete each complex sentence with a subordinating conjunction that tells **when, why,** or **what may happen.**

6. Kristin wrote an article about our graduation _____after_____ it took place. **(when)**

7. I gave her photographs of the ceremony to clip to the article _____before_____ she sent the article to the newspaper. **(when)**

8. She chose the photograph of the class cheering together _____because_____ their faces communicated their mood. **(why)**

9. She will send the photograph with the article _____although_____ they may not publish it. **(what may happen)**

Write It

C. Answer the questions below about ways photographs reveal truth or create bias. Use complex sentences with clauses that act as adverbs.

10. Describe photographs you have seen that revealed the truth about people or events.
I have seen _____.

11. Have you seen photographs that disguised the truth or created bias? Describe them.
_____

12. In which periodicals have you noticed enhanced photographs of people or places?
_____

D. (13–15) Write at least three sentences to tell more about ways photographs reveal or disguise the truth. Use complex sentences with clauses that act as adverbs.

_____
_____
_____
_____
_____

(88) Can a Clause Act Like an Adjective?

Yes, and It Often Begins with *Who*, *That*, or *Which*.

- A **complex sentence** has one independent clause and one dependent clause.

  Students read school | **newspapers that contain sensationalized articles.**

  independent clause   dependent clause

- Some **dependent clauses** act like adjectives and tell more about a noun. They begin with a **relative pronoun**.

  1. Use **who** to tell about a person.

  2. Use **that** for things or people.

  3. Use **which** for things.

- Place an **adjective clause** right after the noun it describes.

  I prefer newspapers **that** contain plain and simple facts.

  I know many other students **who** agree with me.

  I write for the *North High News*, **which** comes out once a month.

Try It

A. Complete each sentence by adding the relative pronoun **who** or **that**.

1. Students always discuss the articles _____that_____ are sensationalized.

2. They don't want to write for newspapers _____that_____ contain exaggerations.

3. I know others _____who_____ think that will make the newspaper boring.

4. The editors will not approve a change _____that_____ will make the paper boring.

B. Read the sentences about newspaper articles. Add an adjective clause to each.

Possible responses:

5. My parents say many newspapers contain articles __that exaggerate details to__ __make them exciting__.

6. All of the students __who go to our school__ know why.

7. Our old school newspaper, __which I read daily__, includes some sensational details.

C. Answer the questions about sensationalized news. Use relative pronouns that introduce adjective clauses.

8. Describe one periodical in which you have read sensationalized news. I have read the periodical _____, which _____.

9. How do you feel about the information in this source? I feel _____.

10. How do you know when an article is sensationalized? _____

11. Do you feel that sensationalizing media is dishonest or necessary? Why? _____

_____

D. (12–15) Write at least four additional sentences about your feelings about sensationalized media. Use adjective clauses in your responses.

_____

_____

_____

_____

Edit It

E. (16–20) Edit the ad. Fix the five mistakes with relative pronouns.

We have made a toothpaste that will change your life!
                    that
It has a taste who makes people leap out of bed every
          ^who
morning. People which feel that brushing their teeth is
              ^
a boring chore will change their minds. Once you use a
              that
toothpaste who sparkles and glows like this one, you will
          ^   who
never change brands. People which use our toothpaste
                              ^
claim it whitens their teeth! Don't wait to try something
that
who will change your life.
^

Proofreader's Marks

Change text:
                who
People which read this
magazine like exciting
news.

See all Proofreader's Marks
on page ix.

89 How Can You Fix a Fragment?

Try Connecting It to a Neighboring Sentence.

> If a fragment is a phrase or a dependent clause, you can often connect it to a nearby sentence.
>
> **Fragment:**   I like to read. About health and medicine.
>
> **Sentence:**   I like to read about health and medicine.
>
> **Fragment:**   Because I love the topic. I read many magazines about health.
>
> **Sentence:**   Because I love the topic, I read many magazines about health.

Try It

A. Fix each fragment. Form a complete complex sentence that includes a dependent and an independent clause.

1. I have read popular magazines. That are interesting but not very scientific. __I have read__ __popular magazines that are interesting but not very scientific.__

2. I like scientific journals. Because they explain conclusions with data. __I like scientific__ __journals because they explain conclusions with data.__

3. Magazines about health often give tips. That are very useful. __Magazines about__ __health often give tips that are very useful.__

B. Turn each fragment into a complete sentence. Add an independent clause.
Possible responses:
4. Although some people dislike popular magazines, __I enjoy them.__

   _____

5. When popular magazines present topics, __they often simplify them for readers.__

   _____

6. Because scientific journals are for scientists, __the average person can't__ __understand them.__

Write It

C. Answer the questions about articles in popular magazines. Avoid using fragments.

7. What popular magazines do you and your friends enjoy reading? My friends and I

_____.

8. What do you find enjoyable about these magazines? These magazines _____

_____.

9. Generally, do you think popular magazines are a reliable or questionable source of information? Why? _____

D. **(10–11)** Write at least two additional sentences about information in popular magazines. Fix any fragments.

_____

_____

_____

_____

Edit It

E. **(12–15)** Edit the ad. Fix the four mistakes with sentence fragments.

My science report examines results found in a survey of genetic traits. These are traits. That are passed from parents to children through genes. I focused on traits that are passed through recessive genes. The gene that results in blue eye color. Is an example of a recessive gene. People who have blue eyes. Received this gene from both parents. Although this does not mean both parents had blue eyes. They both carried the gene for blue eye color.

Proofreader's Marks
Delete:
These are genes that are not dominant.
Add comma:
Although it is rare, one blue and one brown eye is possible.
Do not capitalize:
Other readers prefer popular Magazines.
See all Proofreader's Marks on page ix.

90 Use Complex Sentences

Remember: When you use a variety of sentences, your writing is more interesting.

Expand a simple sentence to a **complex sentence**.

- Add an **adjective clause** to tell more about a noun.
  Use a **relative pronoun** (that, which, who).
  I read the article about genes.
  I read the article about genes, **which is what I want to study in college**.

- Add an **adverb clause** to tell more about an action.
  Use a **subordinating conjunction** (after, although, if, because).
  People check sources on the Internet **if they want the most current news**.

Try It

A. Revise each sentence by adding an adjective or adverb clause. Write **adjective** or **adverb** on the line. Possible responses:

1. Newspapers contain information. _adjective; Newspapers contain information that is quite current._

2. Web sites stay even more current. _adverb; Although newspapers have current information, Web sites stay even more current._

3. Many teenagers have phones. _adjective; Many teenagers have phones that can connect to the Internet._

4. Almost everyone gets news from the Web. _adverb; Almost everyone gets news from the Web because it contains information from around the world._

5. Some teenagers check news updates on their phones. _adverb; Some teenagers check updates on their phones after they read about current events on the Internet._

B. **(6–10) Read the interview about how a teenager receives current information. Choose the correct word to form an adjective or adverb clause.**

Q. What are some ways _____*that*_____ you and your friends receive current
    who / that
    information?

A. We have definite preferences, _____*which*_____ match our personalities.
    who / which
    My friend Shannon gets information from the newspaper. ____*Although*____
    Although / Because
    she feels that technology is helpful, too much can make her life hectic. Antoine,

    _____*who*_____ is in my math class, likes to get information through his
    who / which
    phone. He is able to keep updated _____*because*_____ he stays on top of the news.
    because / if

Write It

C. **Answer the questions about the ways you prefer to receive information. Vary your sentences by using relative and subordinate clauses.**

11. What are some ways you like to receive information? I like to receive information

_____ because _____.

12. Why do you like these ways best? I like these ways best _____.

13. What do these methods reveal about your personality and priorities? _____

14. What are your favorite sources of information? _____

15. What are ways to receive information that you would like to explore? _____

_____

D. **(16–20) Write at least five more sentences that describe ways you prefer to receive information. Vary your sentences by making them complex.**

_____

_____

_____

_____

_____

_____

✔ Capitalize Specific School Courses

- Capitalize the names of courses in school only when they are languages or names of specific courses.

    Are you taking **Spanish** next year?

    I am signed up for **Algebra I**.

- Do not capitalize general course names.

    Melanie uses skills from her **art** class at her after-school job.

    Brett needs to finish his **geometry** homework before basketball practice.

Try It

A. (1–5) Fix the five capitalization errors in the letter. Use proofreader's marks.

Dear Mr. Menendez:

    I am writing to apply for a summer job with your construction company. I am very interested in studying Architecture in college, and I think working for you would be a great experience. I have no problem getting to work early in the morning because I've been waking up before sunrise to do observations for my Astronomy class. I am also familiar with basic construction principles because I've taken several Engineering courses, including introductory AutoCAD and advanced Autodesk Inventor 3D. I promise you that I am a hard worker and will make the most of the experience.

Sincerely,

Faith Jackson

Proofreader's Marks

Capitalize:

    I need help with my french homework.

Do not capitalize:

    I can help you study for your Physics test.

See all Proofreader's Marks on page ix.

B. (6–7) Write at least two sentences about general and specific courses you would like to take at your school. Be sure to use correct rules of capitalization. Sentences will vary.

_____

_____

✔ Use Semicolons and Commas Correctly

- Use a **semicolon** to join two complete sentences that are related.

   Omar works after school; he's a bagger at the supermarket.

   Sierra doesn't want to get a job; however, she needs to earn some money.

- Use a **comma** with a **coordinating conjunction** to join two complete sentences.

   Jessica works at the mall during the week, **and** she is a lifeguard on weekends.

   Derek wants an after-school job, **but** he has football practice every day until 6:00.

   Andrea can get a job as a waitress, **or** she can volunteer at a nursing home.

Coordinating Conjunctions
and (to join like ideas)
but (to join different ideas)
or (to show a choice)

Try It

A. Edit each sentence. Add a semicolon or a comma where necessary. Use proofreader's marks.

8. The new clothing store in town is hiring⌄the managers are looking for high school students to work part-time.

9. Maya and I are walking downtown after school⌄and we're going to fill out applications.

10. I would go with you⌄however, I have soccer practice.

11. You can go tomorrow⌄or you can go on Saturday morning.

12. I would go on Saturday morning⌄but I have a soccer game.

Proofreader's Marks

Add a semicolon:

I have no money⌄ therefore, I need to get a job.

Add a comma:

I'd like to work on weekdays⌄but I'd prefer not to work on weekends.

B. (13–14) Write at least two sentences about your after-school job or activities. Use either a semicolon or a comma with a coordinating conjunction in each sentence. Sentences will vary.

_____

_____

Edit and Proofread

✔ Use Precise Language

- Substitute general words with specific words.

   I got a job at a store.

   I got a job at **the local hardware store**.

- Replace words such as **few**, **many**, and **some** with specific amounts.

   I can earn some money every week.

   I can earn fifty dollars every week.

- Add a word or phrase to provide more information about another word.

   I perform many different tasks.

   I perform **many different tasks, such as helping customers, working the cash register, and stocking shelves**.

Try It

A. Rewrite each sentence. Replace the underlined word or phrase with more precise language or add more precise language to describe it. New sentences will vary.

15. Raul needs <u>some money</u>.

_____

16. He is saving up for <u>something</u>.

_____

17. He wants to apply for <u>a job</u>.

_____

18. Mrs. Turner needs <u>some extra help</u>.

_____

19. She wants to hire someone who can work <u>many hours</u>.

_____

20. She needs someone with <u>a lot of experience</u>.

_____

✓ Build Effective Sentences

- When joining two sentences with a **subordinating conjunction**, make sure the conjunction goes with the less important sentence. That way, the less important sentence supports the main sentence instead of the opposite.

Subordinating Conjunctions
before, when (to show time)
because, so (to show cause and effect)
although, even though (to show opposition)

  Incorrect: Even though I never have enough money, I have a job.

  Correct: Even though I have a job, I never have enough money.

- When combining sentences, keep elements of the new sentence parallel in form. This means they should have the same grammar form.

  Incorrect: Sam enjoys **meeting** new people and **to stock** shelves.

  Correct: Sam enjoys **meeting** new people and **stocking** shelves.

Try It

A. Rewrite each sentence. Correct the placement of the subordinating conjunction, or make the sentence parts parallel.

21. They didn't get enough sleep because they are tired.

   Because they didn't get enough sleep, they are tired.

22. Although I get only seven hours of sleep, I need eight.

   Although I need eight hours of sleep, I only get seven.

23. A lack of sleep can cause depression and being careless.

   A lack of sleep can cause depression and carelessness.

24. When you sleep enough, you feel alert and have high energy.

   When you sleep enough, you feel alert and energetic.

25. Poor sleep results in lower grades and scoring low on tests.

   Poor sleep results in lower grades and test scores.

91 Why Do Verbs Have So Many Forms?

Because They Change to Show When an Action Happens

The tense of a verb shows when an action happens.

Past **Earlier** / **Now** / **Later** Future

Past Tense
visit**ed**

Present Tense
visit
visits

Future Tense
will visit

- **Present tense** verbs tell about actions that happen now or on a regular basis.

    I **visit** my grandparents. I always **go** to their house.

- **Past tense** verbs tell about actions that already happened.
    Add **-ed** to show the past, or use the correct form of an irregular verb.

    I **visited** my grandparents a year ago. I **went** to their house last July.

Present Tense	am, is	are	have, has	go, goes	see, sees
Past Tense	was	were	had	went	saw

- **Future tense** verbs tell about actions that haven't happened yet.

    I **will visit** my grandparents soon. I **will go** to their house next week.

Try It

A. Rewrite each sentence. Change the underlined verb to the past tense.

1. My family <u>lives</u> here. We <u>like</u> this neighborhood. _My family lived here. We liked this neighborhood._

2. I <u>see</u> my grandmother every day. She <u>helps</u> me with my homework. _I saw my grandmother every day. She helped me with my homework._

3. I <u>am</u> happy to live near her. We <u>have</u> a lot of fun together. _I was happy to live near her. We had a lot of fun together._

205

B. Complete each sentence with a verb from the box. Use the correct tense of the verb: past, present, or future. You can use words more than once.

| are | call | come | live | miss | move | stay | visit |

4. Last year, my family _moved_ to New York.

5. My father _came_ here because of a new job.

6. When we left, my grandparents _stayed_ in the Philippines.

7. My sisters and I _were_ very sad the day we left.

8. Now, we _are_ very far from our grandparents.

9–10. A year ago, we _lived_ next door to them. I still _miss_ them.

11–12. They _call_ us every weekend. Next summer, we _will visit_ them.

Write It

C. Answer the questions about moving to a new place. Use past, present, and future tense verbs.

13. Who in your family has moved to a new community? _____

14. Is it difficult to be separated from family members? _____

15. How can you stay in touch with family members? _____

16. Tell about a visit to family members that you have made or might make in the future.

_____

_____

D. (17–20) Write at least four sentences to tell more about family members who live far away. Use past, present, and future tense verbs.

_____

_____

_____

_____

_____

206

92 What If an Action Happened But You're Not Sure When?

Use the Present Perfect Tense to Tell About It.

- If you know when an action happened in the past, use a **past tense** verb.
  Last month, my older brother **traveled** twice for job interviews.

- If you're not sure when a past action happened, use
  a verb in the **present perfect tense**.
  Jeffrey **has traveled** for interviews many times.

- To form the present perfect, use the helping verb **have** or **has** plus the **past participle** of the main verb. For regular verbs, the past participle ends in **-ed**.

Verb	Past Tense	Past Participle
like	liked	liked
shop	shopped	shopped
try	tried	tried

Try It

A. Complete each sentence. Use the past tense or the present perfect tense.

1. Three months ago, Jeffrey _____ moved _____ away.
   moved / has moved

2. Just before he left, he _____ accepted _____ a job in another city.
   accepted / has accepted

3. We _____ have tried _____ to visit him every week.
   tried / have tried

4. The first time we went, I _____ liked _____ his apartment.
   liked / have liked

5. Last Thursday, Mary Jane _____ decided _____ to join us.
   decided / has decided

6. She _____ has visited _____ Jeffrey many times before.
   visited / has visited

207

B. Write the correct past tense or present perfect tense of the verb in parentheses.

7. Over the past month, my parents _____have changed_____ their work schedules. **(change)**

8. Yesterday, my father _____worked_____ until nine o'clock. **(work)**

9. He _____has told_____ us several times that his company is expanding. **(tell)**

10. Last week, my mother's boss _____asked_____ her to work on Saturdays. **(ask)**

11. My mother _____has agreed_____ to his request a few times. **(agree)**

12. Over time, I _____have adjusted_____ to their new schedules. **(adjust)**

13. Last night, I _____shopped_____ for groceries to help out. **(shop)**

14. Then I _____finished_____ my homework. **(finish)**

15. For the past few weeks, we _____have tried_____ to make the best of the situation. **(try)**

Write It

C. Answer the questions about yourself and a recent change in your family. Use past tense and present perfect tense verbs in your sentences.

16. In the last year, what change has occurred in your family? In the last year, _____

_____

_____.

17. What effect has that change had on you? _____

_____

_____.

D. (18–20) Write at least three sentences to tell more about the change in your family. Use past tense and present perfect tense verbs in your sentences.

_____

_____

_____

_____

93 What If a Past Action Is Still Going On?

Then Use the Present Perfect Tense.

- Use the **present perfect tense** to show that an action began in the past and may still be happening.

  Our family **has created** a very successful business.
  (And we are still running this business.)
  We **have enjoyed** our success. (And we are still enjoying our success.)

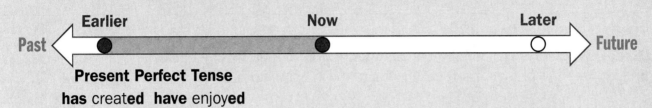

  Present Perfect Tense
  has creat**ed** **have** enjoy**ed**

- A verb in the present perfect tense uses the helping verb **have** or **has** plus the **past participle** of the main verb. For regular verbs, the past participle ends in **-ed**.

Try It

A. (1–5) Write a verb to complete each sentence. Use the present perfect form of the verb in parentheses.

My relatives ___have worked___ as builders for years. **(work)** We ___have earned___ a reputation for good craftsmanship. **(earn)** Sometimes, my uncles ___have argued___ about the business. **(argue)** Then they ___have agreed___ on a plan. **(agree)** Our business ___has lasted___ even through tough times. **(last)**

B. Rewrite each sentence to tell about something that happened in the past. Use the present perfect tense.

6. Uncle Leo and I review the architect's drawings.
   Uncle Leo and I have reviewed the architect's drawings.

7. We discuss the work schedule.
   We have discussed the work schedule.

8. We consult with the building inspector.
   We have consulted with the building inspector.

C. Answer the questions about a business or project that you and your family have worked on together. Use the present perfect tense in some of your sentences.

9. What is a business or project that you have worked on with your family? *My family*

_____

_____ .

10. Did you enjoy working with your family? _____

_____

D. (11–14) Write at least four sentences to tell more about a family business or project. Use the present perfect tense in some of your sentences.

_____

_____

_____

_____

_____

Edit It

E. (15–20) Edit the brochure below. Fix the six mistakes by using the present perfect tense of verbs.

Milbane Motor Company has existed as a family-run car dealership for fifty years. We ~~has focus~~ *have focused* on providing our customers great cars at low prices. We ~~has~~ *have* helped thousands of people find the car of their dreams. Our family ~~has work~~ *has worked* hard to build a business you can trust. We ~~enjoy~~ *have enjoyed* serving the downtown area for many years. We ~~add~~ *have added* many used cars to our lot. Tim, Paul, and Rita Milbane invite you to visit our showroom today and see what we ~~accomplish~~ *have accomplished* over the past five decades.

Proofreader's Marks

Change text:
We ~~earn~~ *have earned* our good reputation over the years.

See all Proofreader's Marks on page ix.

94 Do All Past Participles End in *-ed*?

No, Irregular Verbs Have Special Forms.

- Past participles of irregular verbs have completely new spellings.

	Verb	Past Tense	Past Participle
Forms of *Be*	am, is	was	been
	are	were	been
	give	gave	given
	go	went	gone
	see	saw	seen

- Use **has** or **have** plus the past participle to form the **present perfect tense**.

    My family **has seen** how frail our grandmother has become.

    My parents **have been** very worried about her.

Try It

A. Complete each sentence. Write the present perfect form of the verb in parentheses.

1. My mother ___has gone___ to take care of my grandmother. **(go)**

2. My grandmother ___has been___ sick. **(is)**

3. I ___have seen___ my grandmother only once this year. **(see)**

4. She ___has given___ us many treasures. **(give)**

B. (5–8) Add an irregular verb in the present perfect form to complete each sentence.

Possible responses:
My sisters and I ___have been___ waiting for good news. My father ___has gone___
to help my mother. They ___have given___ my grandmother medicine every four hours.
My parents say that this week ___has been___ hard for them.

C. Answer the questions about different generations of a family helping each other. Use irregular verbs in some of your sentences.

9. How have different generations of your family helped each other? _____

_____

10. What have you done to help if a parent or grandparent is ill? _____

_____

11. What other kinds of help have you given to parents or grandparents? _____

_____

D. (12–15) Write at least three sentences about how your relatives have helped each other. Use irregular verbs in the present perfect tense in some of your sentences.

_____

_____

_____

_____

_____

Edit It

E. (16–20) Edit the letter below. Fix the five mistakes. Use the present perfect tense of the verbs.

Dear Aunt Tanya,

    Ben and I have been eager to share news about our baby

          gone   has

cousin. We have ~~went~~ to visit him three times. Kevin been such a

          ^ have seen   have given ^

good baby. We ~~has see~~ him every day. I ~~has give~~ him his bottle

     has been^

twice! Ben ~~is be~~ even more excited than I have!

Your loving niece,

Janet

Proofreader's Marks

Add text:
    has
She ^ given him a bottle.

Change text:
    have
We ~~has~~ seen the baby.

See all Proofreader's Marks on page ix.

95 Verbs in the Present Perfect Tense

Remember: Use **have** or **has** plus the past participle of a verb to form the present perfect tense.

- The past participle of a **regular verb** ends in **-ed**.
  My sister **has act<u>ed</u>** rudely towards everyone in our family. **(act + -ed)**
  My parents **have arrang<u>ed</u>** for a family meeting. **(arrange [− e] + -ed)**

- The past participle of an **irregular verb** has a completely new spelling.

Verb	Past Participle	Verb	Past Participle
be	been	hold	held
come	come	show	shown
get	got or gotten	take	taken

Try It

A. Complete each sentence. Use the present perfect tense of the verb in parentheses.

1. My sister ___has seemed___ more irritable recently. **(seem)**

2. I ___have been___ upset by her behavior. **(be)**

3. My parents ___have shown___ more patience. **(show)**

4. My sister ___has taken___ clothes from my room. **(take)**

5. My mother ___has come___ home early to talk with her about it. **(come)**

6. I ___have held___ my temper as long as I can. **(hold)**

B. Add a verb in the present perfect form to complete each sentence. Possible responses:

7. For many years, we ___have been___ very close.

8. Lately, my sister ___has treated___ me badly.

9. More recently, she ___has shown___ that she wants to improve our relationship.

213

C. Answer the questions about conflicts. Use the present perfect tense.

10. What has been the cause of a conflict between you and a sibling or parent? _____

_____

11. How have you resolved this conflict? _____

_____

12. What advice has someone given you about how to deal with conflicts? _____

_____

D. (13–15) Write at least three sentences to tell more about how you have handled conflict with a family member. Use the present perfect tense.

_____

_____

_____

_____

_____

Edit It

E. (16–20) Edit the journal entry. Fix the five mistakes.

March 12

Recently, I have been upset with my father.
            have argued
We has argue constantly about his rules. I
    shown ^
have show him that I am responsible. Even my
        ^have
brothers taken my side in the argument. My
            ^have gotten
friends has got tired of me having to be
home so early. They can stay out later. Until
            have been
recently, I has been so close to my father. I
hope we can find a way to resolve this soon.

Proofreader's Marks
Add text: We ^have gone.
Change text: I has ^have been angry.
See all Proofreader's Marks on page ix.

96 How Do You Show Which Past Action Happened First?

Use the Past Perfect Tense.

- Use the **past tense** of a verb to tell about an action that was completed in the past.
  Last week, I **missed** going to the game.

- If you want to show that one past action happened before another, use the **past perfect tense** for the action that happened first.
  I **had planned** to go before my parents **asked** me to help.

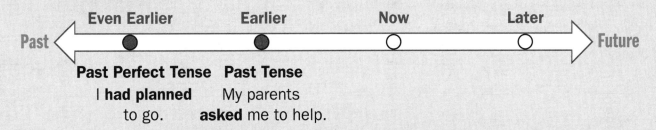

- To form the **past perfect tense**, use **had** plus the **past participle** of the main verb.
  I **told** them I would help although I **had wanted** to see the game.

Try It

A. Write the past perfect tense of the verb in parentheses.

1. I ___had assured___ Lauren that I would go before I agreed to help my parents. **(assure)**

2. Lauren called me at 6 P.M., but I ___had started___ the job. **(start)**

3. I ___had told___ Lauren to go anyway, but she came over to help. **(tell)**

4. We ___had finished___ the job before the game was even over. **(finish)**

B. Complete each sentence by using the past perfect tense. Possible responses:

5. I felt grateful that Lauren ___had helped___ me.

6. Lauren said she ___had wanted___ to spend time with me.

7. I said I ___had enjoyed___ being with her, too.

Write It

C. Answer the questions about helping friends. Use the past perfect tense.

8. Have you ever given up going to an important event to help a friend? Explain. I _____

_____ .

9. How has a friend helped you? _____

10. How has your friend's actions influenced your feelings about the friendship? _____

_____

D. (11–15) Write at least five sentences to tell more about helping or being helped by a friend. Use the past perfect tense.

_____

_____

_____

_____

_____

Edit It

E. (16–20) Edit the journal entry. Fix the five mistakes.

January 23

I had been really nervous about my oral

report before Max ~~help~~ helped me. On Tuesday, I

asked him if I could practice reading my report

aloud to him. Before I ~~talk~~ talked to him, he had

~~arrange~~ arranged to go skating. He changed his plans

and listened to me read. After I ~~have practice~~ had practiced

in front of Max, he said the report was good.

Though I had ~~be~~ been nervous at first, with his help,

I was calm when I presented my report in class.

Proofreader's Marks

Change text:
I had ~~hope~~ hoped to practice.

See all Proofreader's Marks on page ix.

216

97 How Do You Know Which Tense to Use?

Think About When the Action Happened.

- When you tell about the past, you may need to relate actions in time. First use the **past tense** to tell what happened.

  Yesterday, Jamil and Juan **had** a heated discussion about baseball.

- Then use the **past perfect tense** to tell what happened before the discussion.

  They **had discussed** sports often.

- Sometimes a past action may still be going on. That's when you use the **present perfect tense** .

  Jamil and Juan **have disagreed** about sports before.

  They **have attended** many games together since they first **met**.

Try It

A. Complete each sentence. Use the correct form of the verb.

1. Jamil knew Juan from school, but he _____ had known _____ him from the
   knew / had known
   neighborhood first.

2. At school, they had many other friends, although they _____ have been _____
   were / have been
   best friends for many years.

3. Juan played baseball like Jamil, but recently he _____ has realized _____ that
   has realized / had realized
   soccer is more fun for him.

4. Last Friday, Jamil noticed that Juan _____ had chosen _____ to sit with the
   chose / had chosen
   soccer team at lunch.

5. Today, Jamil _____ asked _____ Juan whether he was still mad about their
   asked / had asked
   recent argument.

6. Juan explained that he _____ had wanted _____ to introduce himself to the soccer team.
   has wanted / had wanted

217

B. Write the correct tense of the verb in parentheses. Use the past, past perfect, or present perfect tense.

7. Ann and I talked about how we ____had met____ in math class. **(met)**

8. Last year, Ann ____moved____ to my town. **(move)**

9. Before that, she ____had lived____ in another state. **(live)**

10. Our math teacher ____had divided____ us into groups to study for a test. **(divide)**

11. Ann and I ____were____ in the same group. **(be)**

12. I thought math was hard, but Ann ____had liked____ math since she was little. **(like)**

13. She made math interesting, and we ____have been____ friends ever since. **(be)**

14. We ____have spent____ lots of time together since we met in that group. **(spend)**

Write It

C. Answer the questions about yourself and a good friend. Use verbs in the past, past perfect, and present perfect tenses.

15. Think of a good friend. How did you meet that person? I _____

_____.

16. Did you become friends right away or did it take time? Explain. _____

_____

17. What interests or activities have you shared with this friend? _____

_____

D. (18–20) Write at least three sentences to tell more about how you met or got to know your friend.

_____

_____

_____

_____

218

(98) When Do You Use the Future Perfect Tense?

When You Want to Relate a Future Action to a Future Time

- Sometimes an action that hasn't yet happened depends on another future event. That's when you use the **future perfect tense**.

  Soon **summer will be here**. By then, I **will have finished** my junior year.

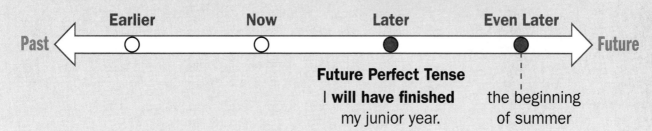

- To form the **future perfect tense**, use **will have** plus the **past participle** of the main verb.

  Before summer comes, I **will have joined** the gymnastics team.

  By next week, Eduardo **will have started** practicing with the swim team.

Try It

A. Complete each sentence. Use the future perfect form of the verb in parentheses.

1. This summer, I _____will have been_____ friends with Eduardo for five years. **(be)**

2. By next year, we _____will have gone_____ to school together for three years. **(go)**

3. We _____will have joined_____ different school teams by the fall. **(join)**

4. Hopefully, by the end of summer, we _____will have stayed_____ friends. **(stay)**

5. Before the summer ends, we _____will have enjoyed_____ some time together. **(enjoy)**

B. Rewrite each sentence to tell about something in the future. Use the future perfect tense.

Possible responses:
6. Eduardo and I watch the movie. _____By tonight, Eduardo and I will have watched the movie._____

7. We laugh at the funny parts together. _____We will have laughed at the funny parts together._____

8. Tony sees a different movie. _____Tony will have seen a different movie._____

Write It

C. Answer the questions about yourself and your friends. Use the future perfect tense.

9. How do you think your friendships might change in the future? In the future, I _____

_____.

10. What events might change a friendship? _____

_____

11. What will you and your friends have done by the end of the school year? _____

_____

D. (12–15) Write at least four sentences about yourself and one or more of your friends. Tell what you think will happen in the future.

_____

_____

_____

_____

_____

Edit It

E. (16–20) Edit the letter. Fix the five mistakes. Use the future perfect tense of the verbs.

Dear Uncle Hector,

  By next Wednesday, I will have competed in the swim meet.
Hopefully, before the meet is over, I ~~got~~ a medal. By the following
will have gotten

will have started
week, I ~~has start~~ rehearsals for my band concert. By the time
the concert night arrives, I ~~rehearsed~~ for about 20 hours. Also,
will have rehearsed

will have missed
I ~~miss~~ a party that's happening that same night. I am so busy, I
don't have much time to spend with my friends. But I hope that
will have had
by the time you read this, I ~~have~~ some time to relax with my family.

Your nephew,

Julio

Proofreader's Marks

Change text:
will have finished
I ~~has finish~~ my work.
    ∧

See all Proofreader's Marks
on page ix.

(99) How Are the Past Perfect and Future Perfect Tenses Alike?

They Both Show How One Action Happens Before Another.

- Use the **past perfect tense** to help your readers know that an action happened even earlier than another past action.

  Before the school year **ended**, I **had transferred** to a new school.

- Use the **future perfect tense** to help your readers know that an action will happen before some other time in the future.

  By the time summer comes, I **will have made** lots of new friends.

Try It

A. Complete each sentence. Use the past perfect or future perfect tense of the verb in parentheses.

1. Before our school closed, I _____ had made _____ many friends. **(make)**

2. When I left the building, I _____ had said _____ good-bye to everyone. **(say)**

3. By next fall, I _____ will have entered _____ a new school in a new neighborhood. **(enter)**

4. By the time I join a team, I _____ will have met _____ some new classmates. **(meet)**

B. Add a verb in the past perfect or future perfect tense to complete each sentence.
Possible responses:

5. At my old school, I _____ had known _____ many teachers.

6. After the first day at my new school, I _____ will have met _____ other teachers.

7. After the first semester, I _____ will have become _____ more comfortable at the new school.

8. Before I changed schools, I _____ had learned _____ to play soccer.

9. By the end of next year, I _____ will have trained _____ with a new coach.

C. Answer the questions about yourself and changes you have or will have experienced. Use verbs in the past perfect or future perfect tense in your sentences.

10. What would happen to your friendships if you had to change schools? _____

_____

11. Describe how a student makes new friends after transferring to a different school.

_____

_____

D. (12–15) Write at least four sentences about what you might do at a new school or what you did at an old school. Use verbs in the past perfect or future perfect tense in your sentences.

_____

_____

_____

_____

_____

_____

E. (16–20) Edit the letter. Fix the five mistakes with verbs. Use the past, past perfect, or future perfect tense of the verbs.

Dear Isabella,

    By the time you read this, I will have finished the fall semester at school. Before Thanksgiving, my parents ~~have~~ [will have found] a place for us to live in Chicago. Soon, Nancy and I ~~say~~ [will have said] good-bye to our neighborhood friends. Last week, we ~~pack~~ [packed] up lots of household items to donate to a local thrift store. By the time we were done, I ~~will have~~ [had] gotten rid of my old bike. Before we are all moved in, Dad says he ~~buys~~ [will have bought] me a new one!

Your friend,

Carlos

Proofreader's Marks

Change text:
  will have packed
We ~~will pack~~ all our
books.

See all Proofreader's Marks on page ix.

(100) Write with the Perfect Tenses

Remember: Use the present perfect, past perfect, and future perfect tenses to show how actions are related in time. Study the chart.

Tense	When Do You Use It?	Examples
Present Perfect	For actions that began in the past and are still going on	Tensho **has helped** me since we became good friends.
	For actions that happened at an unknown past time	Our fathers **have worked** together a lot.
Past Perfect	For actions completed before another past action	Before I **met** Tensho, I **had hoped** to find a best friend.
Future Perfect	For actions that will happen before a future time	**By fall**, we **will have been** friends for two years.

Try It

A. Complete each sentence. Use one of the perfect tenses of the verb in parentheses.

1. Tensho _____has asked_____ me for help. **(ask)**

2. He _____has helped_____ me many times. **(help)**

3. I _____have wanted_____ to do something to repay him. **(want)**

4. Before Tensho's bike broke, he _____had used_____ it to get to his job after school. **(use)**

5. I _____have offered_____ him my bike until his is repaired. **(offer)**

6. I _____have walked_____ home from school all week. **(walk)**

7. By next weekend, the repair shop _____will have fixed_____ his bike. **(fix)**

B. Choose words from each column to build five sentences about helping a friend. You can use words more than once. Possible responses:

Tensho I The repairman We	have been had been has helped has ridden will have fixed	the bike by Saturday. me many times. best friends for two years. worried about getting to work. my bike all week.

8. Tensho has ridden my bike all week.

9. Tensho had been worried about getting to work.

10. The repairman will have fixed the bike by Saturday.

11. Tensho has helped me many times.

12. We have been best friends for two years.

Write It

C. Answer the questions about yourself and a good friend. Use perfect tenses.

13. How has your friend shown generosity when you needed help? _____

14. How will you have helped a friend by the end of the school year? _____

_____

15. Have you learned to trust your friend, based on his or her actions? Why or why not?

_____

D. (16–20) Write at least five sentences to tell about ways that you and a friend help each other. Use perfect tenses in your sentences.

_____

_____

_____

_____

_____

_____

101 Can a Verb Act Like an Adjective?

Yes, When It is a Participle

- Verbs have **four principal parts**. For example:

Present	Present Participle	Past	Past Participle
drive	driving	drove	driven
excite	exciting	excited	excited

- Many **verbs** are made up of a **helping verb** and a **participle**.

  Present Participle: My mother **is driving** to the store again.

  Past Participle: She **has driven** around all morning getting supplies.

- A **participle** can act as an adjective to describe a noun or pronoun.

  Mr. Powell is a **driven** man who tirelessly helps his neighbors.

  Excited, the neighbors look forward to the block party.

Try It

A. Combine sentences. Move the underlined participle to tell about a noun or a pronoun in the other sentence. Write the new sentence. Possible responses:

1. Warm weather brings the neighbors outside. They are <u>waiting</u>.

   Warm weather brings the waiting neighbors outside.

2. The neighbors set up tables and chairs. They are <u>excited</u>.

   Excited, the neighbors set up tables and chairs.

3. The block party includes new and old neighbors. It is <u>welcoming</u>.

   The welcoming block party includes new and old neighbors.

4. The children greet their friends. They are <u>running</u>.

   Running, the children greet their friends.

5. The teenagers form a large group. They are <u>dancing</u>.

   The dancing teenagers form a large group.

B. Complete each sentence. Use the present participle or the past participle of the verb in parentheses as an adjective.

6. _____Smiling_____, Betsy asks Joey to perform. **(smile)**

7–8. _____Thrilled_____, Joey sings. **(thrill)** The _____pleased_____ crowd listens. **(please)**

9. _____Clapping_____, the neighbors praise Joey's performance. **(clap)**

Write It

C. Answer the questions. Use present and past participles as adjectives.

10. What yearly celebration or tradition do you enjoy in your community? _____

_____

11. How do most people feel about the celebration? _____

_____

D. (12–16) Now write at least five sentences to tell more about the community event. Use participles as adjectives.

_____

_____

_____

_____

Edit It

E. (17–20) Edit the letter below. Fix the four mistakes. Use present or past participles.

Dear Nora,

Today, our neighborhood had an exciting street fair. We
thought it might be ruined by the ~~drive~~ driving winds. ~~Grin~~ Grinning, Mr. Pearson
said not to worry. A band played ~~boom~~ booming rock music. We got
there early. ~~Exhaust~~ Exhausted, we finally left at 5 o'clock!

Your pal,

Ali

Proofreader's Marks

Change text:
              Shouting
~~Shout~~, he called me over.

See all Proofreader's Marks
on page ix.

226

102 What Are Participial Phrases?

Phrases That Start with a Participle

- A **participle** is a verb form, but it can act like an adjective to describe a noun or a pronoun. It can stand alone or come at the start of a **phrase**. A participle often ends in **-ing**.

  Working, Maria helps clean up trash in the neighborhood.

  Seeing the activity, Thomas joins the people **cleaning** the neighborhood.

- You can create a **participial phrase** to combine two sentences. If the phrase begins a sentence, use a comma (**,**) after the phrase.

  Maria helps with the clean-up. Maria works hard.

  Helping with the clean-up, Maria works hard.

- Place a participial phrase close to the noun or pronoun that it describes.

  Not OK: Thomas picks up soda bottles **bending** over the curb.

  OK: **Bending** over the curb, Thomas picks up soda bottles.

Try It

A. Use a participial phrase to combine sentences. Write the new sentence. Don't forget the comma after a participial phrase at the start of a sentence. Possible responses:

1. Mr. Rummel organizes the clean-up. Mr. Rummel assigns each neighbor a job.
   Organizing the clean-up, Mr. Rummel assigns each neighbor a job.

2. Mrs. Rummel greets each neighbor. Mrs. Rummel hands out tools and garbage bags.
   Greeting each neighbor, Mrs. Rummel hands out tools and garbage bags.

3. Thomas roams the neighborhood. Thomas gathers lots of bottles and cans.
   Roaming the neighborhood, Thomas gathers lots of bottles and cans.

4. Maria watches people. They are picking up paper and other debris.
   Maria watches people picking up paper and other debris.

5. Delia smiles as she works. Delia plants many flowers.
   Smiling as she works, Delia plants many flowers.

B. Choose from the participles in the box to complete each sentence. Possible responses:

exhausted	giggling	helping	looking	resting	sweeping

6. ___Exhausted___, Mr. Rodriguez sleeps in a chair.

7. Mrs. Rummel watches the children ___helping___ with the clean-up.

8. ___Sweeping___ the sidewalk, Mrs. Bianco meets her neighbors.

9. She notices the whole neighborhood ___looking___ much better.

10. ___Resting___, the adults admire the successful clean-up.

11. ___Giggling___, the children race around the tidy playground.

Write It

C. Answer the questions about keeping neighborhoods clean. Use participial phrases in your answers.

12. Is there a clean-up in your neighborhood every year? _____

13. What kinds of jobs do people do in a neighborhood clean-up? _____

_____

14. Is it important for people to work together to keep their neighborhood looking nice? Why or why not? _____

_____

15. How does having a clean neighborhood benefit the people who live there? _____

_____

D. (16–20) Write at least five sentences to tell more about how you and your neighbors keep your neighborhood clean. Use participial phrases in your sentences.

_____

_____

_____

_____

_____

103 How Can You Add Details to Your Sentences?

Use a Participial Phrase.

- A **participial phrase** begins with a **participle**.
  It acts like an adjective to describe a noun or a pronoun.

  1. The present participle for all verbs ends in **-ing**.

     Growing each year, my city has people from many countries.

  2. The past participle of a regular verb ends in **-ed**.
     An irregular verb has a special form.

Verb	Past	Past Participle
appreciate	appreciated	appreciated
choose	chose	chosen

     This neighborhood is a community **appreciated for its diversity**.

     Chosen by the community, our mayor is Chinese.

- You can use a participial phrase to add details to your sentences.

  Emigrating from **Argentina**, my father moved here three years ago.

Try It

A. Add a participial phrase to each sentence. Change the verb in parentheses to a present or past participle to start the phrase. Possible responses:

1. Our street has many buildings ___inhabited by South Americans___. **(inhabit)**

2. Mrs. Carvalho is a samba dancer ___respected for her skill___. **(respect)**

3. ___Coming from different countries___, people have varied backgrounds. **(come)**

4. ___Sharing their games___, the children learn about different cultures. **(share)**

5. Tina taught us a game ___played in her country___. **(play)**

B. Complete each sentence about a diverse community. Use the correct form of the participle.

6. _____Cooking_____ their favorite foods, my classmates present dishes from their
   <u>Cooking/Cooked</u>
   cultures.

7. Badia's family brings us couscous _____mixed_____ with vegetables.
   <u>mixing/mixed</u>

8. _____Telling_____ stories about her grandmother, Sophia serves us pasta.
   <u>Telling/Told</u>

9. Dien gives us dumplings _____eaten_____ in Vietnam.
   <u>eating/eaten</u>

10. I bring steak _____prepared_____ Argentinean style.
    <u>preparing/prepared</u>

11. _____Filled_____ with spices, Romero's pastries are delicious.
    <u>Filling/Filled</u>

Write It

C. Answer the questions about people in your community. Use participial phrases.

12. What cultures are represented in your community? _____

_____

13. What new foods have friends from other cultures shared with you? _____

_____

14. What foods would you share from your culture? _____

_____

15. What other aspects of your heritage would you share with your community? _____

_____

**D. (16–20) Write at least five sentences to tell more about the benefits of living
in a multicultural community. Use participial phrases.**

_____

_____

_____

_____

_____

104 What Is a "Dangling Participle"?

It's a Participle That Describes the Wrong Word.

- Always place a **participial phrase** by the word it describes.
  Sometimes you can just move the phrase to fix the problem.

  Not OK: I have lived here a long time, **finding this city wonderful**.

  OK: **Finding this city wonderful**, I have lived here a long time.

- Sometimes you need to rephrase the sentence and include a word for the participle to describe.

  Not OK: **Watching soccer**, our city's players had skills.

  OK: **Watching soccer**, Katya saw the skills of our city's players.

Try It

A. Fix each dangling participle. Write the sentence correctly.   Possible responses:

1. Katya tells us about the soccer team beaming with pride.
    Beaming with pride, Katya tells us about the soccer team.

2. She shows us pictures of the winning goal returning from the latest game.
    Returning from the latest game, she shows us pictures of the winning goal.

3. We recognized a player from our neighborhood looking at the pictures.
    Looking at the pictures, we recognized a player from our neighborhood.

4. The coach unites the players believing in teamwork.
    Believing in teamwork, the coach unites the players.

5. The soccer team is everyone's favorite winning the championship.
    Winning the championship, the soccer team is everyone's favorite.

6. Cheering at games, our team wins.
    Cheering at games, I am happy when our team wins.

B. (7–11) Complete each sentence. Make sure you have included a word or words for the participle to describe. Possible responses:

Kicking deftly, _____Ramon sees that_____ the ball has reached the goal. Screaming wildly, _____the fans realize that_____ the game is won. Running across the field, _____the team knows that_____ the crowd is happy. Breathing a sigh of relief, _____the coach sees that_____ his team is elated. Bursting with pride, _____Ramon's parents think_____ their son is a great soccer player.

Write It

C. Answer the questions about sports and other events that bring your community together. Use participial phrases correctly.

12. What sports events make you proud of your community? _____

_____

13. What other events (holidays, other traditional celebrations, and so on) in your community are you proud of? _____

_____

14. Do most people in your community attend these events? _____

_____

15. Describe your favorite community event. _____

_____

D. (16–20) Write at least five sentences to tell about one or more community events that you are proud of. Use participial phrases correctly.

_____

_____

_____

_____

_____

Name _____   Date _____

⑯ Enrich Your Sentences

Remember: A **participle** is a verb form that can act as an adjective.
A **participial phrase** begins with a participle. Participles and participial phrases describe nouns and pronouns.

- A **participle** ends in **-ing** or **-ed**, or it has a special form. It can stand alone, or it can come at the start of a **participial phrase**.

  Worried new students enter the classroom.

  Showing friendliness, my classmates welcomed the refugees.

  Amazed by their new surroundings, the students explore the school.

- You can use participial phrases to combine or expand sentences.

  I admired the new students. I wanted to get to know them better.

  Admiring the new students, I wanted to get to know them better.

Try It

A. Use a participial phrase to combine each pair of sentences.

1. Nina left her grandparents. She emigrated from Bosnia. _Leaving her grandparents,_ Nina emigrated from Bosnia.

2. She was filled with sadness. She missed her homeland. _Filled with sadness, she_ missed her homeland.

3. Ahmed arrived from Africa. He quickly learned English. _Arriving from Africa, Ahmed_ quickly learned English.

4. We were inspired by their courage. Everyone rallied around the new students. _Inspired_ by their courage, everyone rallied around the new students.

B. Complete each sentence about new students. Use the correct form of the participle.

5. ____Talking____ slowly, Nina tells us her story.
    Talking/Talked

6. ____Sitting____ together, Nina and Ahmed discuss their new school.
    Sitting/Sat

7. Ahmed is a friendly teen ____known____ for his humor.
    knowing/known

233

Write It

C. Answer the questions about an inspiring student. Tell how you are inspired by this person. Use participles and participial phrases correctly.

8. Is there a student in your school whom you find especially inspiring? _____

_____

9. What makes this person so remarkable? _____

_____

10. What is a fascinating detail about this person's life? _____

_____

D. (11–14) Write at least four sentences to tell about an inspiring student. Use participles and participial phrases.

_____

_____

_____

_____

Edit It

E. (15–20) Edit the letter. Fix the six mistakes with participles.

Dear Parents and Students:

Building on last year's success, the Student Outreach Group has had another tremendous year. This year's students are a dynamic group distinguishing [distinguished] by their diversity. Represented [Representing] seven countries, they bring new viewpoints to our community. Used [Using] their talents, our students tried to make newcomers feel welcome. Created [Creating] opportunities for students to mingle was a priority. Describe [Described] as a home away from home, the Student Center is a success. Inspiring [Inspired] by new students, many older students have joined our group.

Sincerely yours,

Vice Principal Kristina Hagopian

Proofreader's Marks

Change text:
~~Surprising~~ Surprised by their welcome, the students smiled.

See all Proofreader's Marks on page ix.